LANGUAGE AND LANGUAGE LEA

Chomsky: Selected Readings

LANGUAGE AND LANGUAGE LEARNING

General Editors: RONALD MACKIN *and* PETER STREVENS

Chomsky: Selected Readings

Edited by
J. P. B. ALLEN and *PAUL VAN BUREN*

London
OXFORD UNIVERSITY PRESS
NEW YORK   TORONTO

Oxford University Press, Ely House, London W.1

GLASGOW NEW YORK TORONTO MELBOURNE WELLINGTON

CAPE TOWN IBADAN NAIROBI DAR ES SALAAM LUSAKA ADDIS ABABA

DELHI BOMBAY CALCUTTA MADRAS KARACHI LAHORE DACCA

KUALA LUMPUR SINGAPORE HONG KONG TOKYO

Library Edition ISBN 0 19 437114 X

Paperback Edition ISBN 0 19 437046 1

© Oxford University Press, 1971

First published 1971

Fourth impression 1975

P
27
.C5

ACKNOWLEDGEMENTS

The editors and publishers wish to thank the following for permission
to use extracts from the sources mentioned:

Mouton and Company n.v. (*Topics in the Theory of Generative Grammar
and Syntactic Structures*); Massachusetts Institute of Technology Press
(*Aspects of the Theory of Syntax*); John Wiley and Sons Limited (*Formal
Analysis of Natural Languages*); Harcourt, Brace and World, Inc.
(*Language and Mind*); The Society for Research in Child Development,
Inc. (*The Acquisition of Language*); Linguistic Society of America (*A
Review of B. F. Skinner's Verbal Behavior*); The Northeast Conference on
the Teaching of Foreign Languages (*Linguistic Theory*); The National
Council of Teachers (*The Current Scene in Linguistics: Present Directions*).

75-21877

PRINTED IN GREAT BRITAIN BY HEADLEY BROTHERS LTD
109 KINGSWAY LONDON WC2B 6PX AND ASHFORD KENT

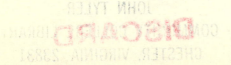

CONTENTS

Editors' Preface

Chomsky's approach to linguistic description became widely known as a result of the publication of *Syntactic Structures* in 1957. In the twelve years that have elapsed since then, transformational-generative grammar—'TG' for short—has established itself as one of the most vigorous and exciting movements in modern linguistics, and one which many people believe has far-reaching implications for the study of human cognitive processes. The aim of this book is to present the main outlines of transformational theory, using as far as possible Chomsky's own words, but arranged in such a way that a non-specialist will have no difficulty in following the text. The topics covered include syntax, phonology, semantics and language acquisition. In the final section, some of the implications of transformational theory for language teaching are considered.

Why 'transformational' and why 'generative'? We hope that these questions will be fully answered during the course of the book, but some explanation is due at the outset. Traditionally, the task of linguistic description is to specify the rules that relate strings of speech sounds to their semantic interpretation, and to do so for an infinite number of cases; in other words, to explain a speaker's intrinsic language 'competence' or knowledge. However, traditional grammars, although meticulous in their discussion of the various form-classes, fail to specify in sufficient detail how the many different components of sentences combine to yield well-formed sentence structures. To a large extent this information has to be provided by the reader's linguistic intuition. As a result we have grammars which attempt to explain the nature of a speaker's linguistic knowledge, but which have to appeal to that very knowledge in order to make good their deficiencies. The only way to avoid this predicament is to require that the rules of the grammar be fully explicit, thus enabling the grammar to specify the structure of sentences independently of a reader's linguistic knowledge. One way of stating this requirement is to say that the predictions afforded by the grammar should be an automatic consequence of its axioms and rules. Another way of stating it is to say that the grammar must be specifiable in the form of a system of rules which will generate all and only the grammatical sentences of a language.

According to Chomsky, the syntactic description of sentences has two aspects: surface structure, and a far more abstract deep structure. Generally speaking, surface structure is the aspect of description that determines the phonetic form of sentences, while deep structure determines semantic interpretation*. The rules that express the relation of deep and surface structure in sentences are called 'grammatical transformations'; hence the term 'transformational-generative grammar'.

It must be clearly understood that current work in generative linguistics is essentially theoretical in nature. It is not motivated by an interest in computers or any other kind of engineering, nor does it constitute an attempt to propagate a new and obscure branch of mathematics. The main purpose of the research is to suggest an explanatory hypothesis concerning the nature of language and ultimately of human thought. Further, the theory of language presented in this book is 'quite explicitly and self-consciously mentalistic', not in the disparaging sense of the word employed by Bloomfield, who saw mentalism in linguistics as an appeal to the occult and the negation of empirical scientific method, but in the sense that a theory of language is to be regarded as a partial theory of the human mind. It follows that human beings, as the users of language in all its aspects, should form the explanatory and empirical domain of linguistic theory. Accordingly, in the context of generative linguistics we are concerned with data not for its own sake but as evidence for the existence of certain organizing principles in the mind which make it possible for a speaker to use language creatively.

The following readings have been selected from a variety of books and articles representing the main outlines of Chomsky's work during the last twelve years. After each extract the title of the original source, together with page numbers, is given. At certain points some editorial commentary was necessary in order to provide a smooth transition between texts. In such cases the editorial material is enclosed by square brackets. Where the editors have contributed the introductory sections of chapters, the initials 'A, B' (for Allen and van Buren) appear in brackets after the relevant sections. In the same way, footnotes are marked 'C' for Chomsky and 'A, B' for Allen and van Buren.

* In some cases surface structure may contribute to semantic interpretation. See section 5.1.

In the section on phonology the phonetic notation used by Chomsky differs from that used by the editors. It was thought better that these discrepancies should be allowed to remain, since the two notations refer to different dialects of English, and any attempt to convert one notation into another would incur the risk of misrepresentation.

The technique of selection has necessitated many small omissions and some manipulation of the cross-paragraph references in the extracts from Chomsky's work. Rather than break up the text with square brackets and rows of dots, we have allowed these modifications to pass without comment. While we feel that this is permissible in a book that is intended to be an introduction rather than a definitive text, reference to the originals is recommended for those readers who wish to make a detailed study of Chomsky's work.

We are very grateful to Noam Chomsky for reading through the manuscript at various stages, and for making a number of valuable suggestions which have been incorporated into the text. John Lyons, Gill Brown and Ruth Clark have also been kind enough to read parts of the book in manuscript; we are deeply indebted to them for their assistance. Any imperfections that remain are, of course, ours alone.

J. P. B. ALLEN
PAUL VAN BUREN

Department of Linguistics, Edinburgh
June 1970

1 Basic Principles

1.1 *Introductory*

Two major traditions can be distinguished in modern linguistic theory:
one is the tradition of 'universal' or 'philosophical grammar', which
flourished in the seventeenth and eighteenth centuries; the second is
the tradition of structural or descriptive linguistics, which reached the
high point of its development perhaps fifteen or twenty years ago.
I think that a synthesis of these two major traditions is possible, and
that it is, to some extent, being achieved in current work. Before
approaching the problem of synthesis, I would like to sketch briefly—
and, necessarily, with some oversimplification—what seems to me to
be the most significant features in these two traditions.

As the name indicates, universal grammar was concerned with
general features of language structure rather than with particular
idiosyncrasies. Particularly in France, universal grammar developed in
part in reaction to an earlier descriptivist tradition which held that the
only proper task for the grammarian was to present data, to give a
kind of 'natural history' of language (specifically, of the 'cultivated
usage' of the court and the best writers). In contrast, universal grammarians urged that the study of language should be elevated from the
level of 'natural history' to that of 'natural philosophy'; hence the
term 'philosophical grammar', 'philosophical' being used, of course,
in essentially the sense of our term 'scientific'. Grammar should not
be merely a record of the data of usage, but, rather, should offer an
explanation for such data. It should establish general principles,
applicable to all languages and based ultimately on intrinsic properties
of the mind, which would explain how language is used and why it
has the particular properties to which the descriptive grammarian
chooses, irrationally, to restrict his attention.

Universal grammarians did not content themselves with merely
stating this goal. In fact, many generations of scholars proceeded to
develop a rich and far-reaching account of the general principles of

language structure, supported by whatever detailed evidence they could find from the linguistic materials available to them. On the basis of these principles, they attempted to explain many particular facts, and to develop a psychological theory dealing with certain aspects of language use, with the production and comprehension of sentences.

The tradition of universal grammar came to an abrupt end in the nineteenth century, for reasons that I will discuss directly. Furthermore, its achievements were very rapidly forgotten, and an interesting mythology developed concerning its limitations and excesses. It has now become something of a cliché among linguists that universal grammar suffered from the following defects: (*a*) it was not concerned with the sounds of speech, but only with writing; (*b*) it was based primarily on a Latin model, and was, in some sense 'prescriptive'; (*c*) its assumptions about language structure have been refuted by modern 'anthropological linguistics'. In addition, many linguists, though not all, would hold that universal grammar was misguided in principle in its attempt to provide explanations rather than mere description of usage, the latter being all that can be contemplated by the 'sober scientist'.

The first two criticisms are quite easy to refute; the third and fourth are more interesting. Even a cursory glance at the texts will show that phonetics was a major concern of universal grammarians, and that their phonetic theories were not very different from our own. Nor have I been able to discover any confusion of speech and writing. The belief that universal grammar was based on a Latin model is rather curious. In fact, the earliest studies of universal grammar, in France, were a part of the movement to raise the status of the vernacular, and are concerned with details of French that often do not even have any Latin analogue.

As to the belief that modern 'anthropological linguistics' has refuted the assumptions of universal grammar, this is not only untrue, but, for a rather important reason, could not be true. The reason is that universal grammar made a sharp distinction between what we may call 'deep structure' and 'surface structure'. The deep structure of a sentence is the abstract underlying form which determines the meaning of the sentence; it is present in the mind but not necessarily represented directly in the physical signal. The surface structure of a sentence is the actual organization of the physical signal into phrases of varying size, into words of various categories, with certain particles, inflections, arrangement, and so on. The fundamental assumption of the universal grammarians was that languages scarcely differ at the level of deep structure—which reflects the basic properties of thought and conception—but that they may vary widely at the much less interesting level of surface structure. But modern anthropological linguistics does not attempt to deal with deep structure and its relations to surface structure. Rather, its attention is limited to surface structure—to the phonetic form of an utterance and its organization into units of varying size. Consequently, the information that it provides has no direct bearing on the hypotheses concerning deep structure postulated by the universal grammarians. And, in fact, it seems to me that what information is now available to us suggests not that they went too far in assuming universality of underlying structure, but that they may have been much too cautious and restrained in what they proposed.

The fourth criticism of universal grammar—namely, that it was misguided in seeking explanations in the first place—I will not discuss. It seems to me that this criticism is based on a misunderstanding of the nature of all rational inquiry. There is particular irony in the fact that this criticism should be advanced with the avowed intention of making linguistics 'scientific'. It is hardly open to question that the natural sciences are concerned precisely with the problem of explaining phenomena, and have little use for accurate description that is un- related to problems of explanation.

I think that we have much to learn from a careful study of what was achieved by the universal grammarians of the seventeenth and eighteenth centuries. It seems to me, in fact, that contemporary linguistics would do well to take their concept of language as a point of departure for current work. Not only do they make a fairly clear and well-founded distinction between deep and surface structure, but they also go on to study the nature of deep structure and to provide valuable hints and insights concerning the rules that relate the abstract underlying mental structures to surface form, the rules that we would now call 'grammatical transformations'. What is more, universal grammar developed as part of a general philosophical tradition that provided deep and important insights, also largely forgotten, into the use and acquisition of language, and, furthermore, into problems of perception and acquisition of knowledge in general. These insights can be exploited and developed. The idea that the study of language should proceed within the framework of what we might nowadays call 'cognitive psychology' is sound. There is much truth in the traditional view that language provides the most effective means for studying the nature and mechanisms of the human mind, and that only within this context can we perceive the larger issues that determine the directions in which the study of language should develop.

The tradition of universal grammar came to an end more than a century ago. Several factors combined to lead to its decline. For one thing, the problems posed were beyond the scope of the technique and understanding then available. The problem of formulating the rules that determine deep structures and relate them to surface structures, and the deeper problem of determining the general abstract characteristics of these rules, could not be studied with any precision, and discussion therefore remained at the level of hints, examples, and vaguely formulated intentions. In particular, the problem of rule-governed creativity in language simply could not be formulated with sufficient precision to permit research to proceed very far. A second reason for the decline of traditional linguistic theory lies in the remarkable successes of Indo-European comparative linguistics in the nineteenth century. These achievements appeared to dwarf the accomplishments of universal grammar, and led many linguists to scoff at the 'metaphysical' and 'airy pronouncements' of those who were attempting to deal with a much wider range of problems—and at that particular stage of the development of linguistic theory, were discussing these topics in a highly inconclusive fashion. Looking back now, we can see quite clearly that the concept of language employed by the Indo-European comparativists was an extremely primitive one. It was, however, well-suited to the tasks at hand. It is, therefore, not too surprising that this concept of language, which was then extended and developed by the structural and descriptive linguists of the twentieth century, became almost completely dominant, and that the older tradition of linguistic theory was largely swept aside and forgotten. This is hardly a unique instance in intellectual history.

Structural linguistics is a direct outgrowth of the concepts that emerged in Indo-European comparative study, which was primarily concerned with language as a system of phonological units that undergo systematic modification in phonetically determined contexts. Structural linguistics reinterpreted this concept for a fixed state of a language, investigated the relations among such units and the patterns they form, and attempted with varying success, to extend the same kind of analysis to 'higher levels' of linguistic structure. Its fundamental assumption is that procedures of segmentation and classification, applied to data in a systematic way, can isolate and identify all types of elements that function in a particular language along with the constraints that they obey. A catalogue of these elements, their relations, and their restrictions of 'distribution', would, in most structuralist views, constitute a full grammar of the language.

Structural linguistics has very real accomplishments to its credit. To me, it seems that its major achievement is to have provided a factual and a methodological basis that makes it possible to return to the problems that occupied the traditional universal grammarians with some hope of extending and deepening their theory of language structure and language use. Modern descriptive linguistics has enormously enriched the range of factual material available, and has provided entirely new standards of clarity and objectivity. Given this advance in precision and objectivity, it becomes possible to return, with new hope for success, to the problem of constructing the theory of a particular language—its grammar—and to the still more ambitious study of the general theory of language. On the other hand, it seems to me that the substantive contributions to the theory of language structure are few, and that, to a large extent, the concepts of modern linguistics constitute a retrogression as compared with universal grammar. One real advance has been in universal phonetics—I refer here particularly to the work of Jakobson. Other new and important insights might also be cited. But in general, the major contributions of structural linguistics seem to me to be methodological rather than substantive. These methodological contributions are not limited to a raising of the standards of precision. In a more subtle way, the idea that language can be studied as a formal system, a notion which is developed with force and effectiveness in the work of Harris and Hockett, is of particular significance. It is, in fact, this general insight and the techniques that emerged as it developed that have made it possible, in the last few years, to approach the traditional problems once again. Specifically, it is now possible to study the problem of rule-governed creativity in natural language, the problem of constructing grammars that explicitly generate deep and surface structures and express the relations between them, and the deeper problem of determining the universal conditions that limit the form and organization of rules in the grammar of a human language. When these problems are clearly formulated and studied, we are led to a conception of language not unlike that suggested in universal grammar. Furthermore, I think that we are led to conclusions regarding mental processes of very much the sort that were developed, with care and insight, in the rationalist philosophy of mind that provided the intellectual background for universal grammar. It is in this sense that I think we can look forward to a productive synthesis of the two major traditions of linguistic research.

If this point of view is correct in essentials, we can proceed to outline the problems facing the linguist in the following way. He is, first of all, concerned to report data accurately. What is less obvious, but nonetheless correct, is that the data will not be of particular interest to him in itself, but rather only insofar as it sheds light on the grammar of the language from which it is drawn, where by the 'grammar of a language' I mean the theory that deals with the mechanisms of sentence construction, which establish a sound-meaning relation in this language. At the next level of study, the linguist is concerned to give a factually accurate formulation of this grammar, that is, a correct formulation of the rules that generate deep and surface structures and interrelate them, and the rules that give a phonetic interpretation of surface structures and a semantic interpretation of deep structures. But, once again, this correct statement of the grammatical principles of a language is not primarily of interest in itself, but only insofar as it sheds light on the more general question of the nature of language; that is, the nature of universal grammar. The primary interest of a correct grammar is that it provides the basis for substantiating or refuting a general theory of linguistic structure which establishes general principles concerning the form of grammar.

Continuing one step higher in level of abstraction, a universal grammar—a general theory of linguistic structure that determines the form of grammar—is primarily of interest for the information it provides concerning innate intellectual structure. Specifically, a general theory of this sort itself must provide a hypothesis concerning innate intellectual structure of sufficient richness to account for the fact that the child acquires a given grammar on the basis of the data available to him. More generally, both a grammar of a particular language and a general theory of language are of interest primarily because of the insight they provide concerning the nature of mental processes, the mechanisms of perception and production, and the mechanisms by which knowledge is acquired. There can be little doubt that both specific theories of particular languages and the general theory of linguistic structure provide very relevant evidence for anyone concerned with these matters; to me it seems quite obvious that it is within this general framework that linguistic research finds its intellectual justification.

The Current Scene in Linguistics: Present Directions, 3–7*

1.2 *The goals of linguistic theory*

A distinction must be made between what the speaker of a language knows implicitly (what we may call his *competence*) and what he does (his *performance*). A grammar, in the traditional view, is an account of competence. It describes and attempts to account for the ability of a speaker to understand an arbitrary sentence of his language and to produce an appropriate sentence on a given occasion. If it is a pedagogic grammar, it attempts to provide the student with this ability; if a linguistic grammar, it aims to discover and exhibit the mechanisms that make this achievement possible. The competence of the speaker-hearer can, ideally, be expressed as a system of rules that relate signals to semantic interpretations of these signals. The problem for the grammarian is to discover this system of rules; the problem for linguistic theory is to discover general properties of any system of rules that may serve as the basis for a human language, that is, to elaborate in detail what we may call, in traditional terms, the general *form of language* that underlies each particular realization, each particular natural language.

Performance provides evidence for the investigation of competence. At the same time, a primary interest in competence entails no disregard for the facts of performance and the problem of explaining these facts. On the contrary, it is difficult to see how performance can be seriously studied except on the basis of an explicit theory of the competence that underlies it, and, in fact, contributions to the understanding of performance have largely been by-products of the study of grammars that represent competence.

Notice, incidentally, that a person is not generally aware of the rules that govern sentence-interpretation in the language that he knows; nor, in fact, is there any reason to suppose that the rules can be brought to consciousness. Furthermore, there is no reason to expect him to be fully aware even of the empirical consequences of these internalized rules—that is, of the way in which signals are assigned

* Reference to page numbers in Reibel and Schane (1969) see page 167.

semantic interpretations by the rules of the language that he knows
(and, by definition, knows perfectly). It is important to realize that
there is no paradox in this; in fact, it is precisely what should be
expected.

Current work in generative grammar has adopted this traditional
framework of interests and concerns. It attempts to go beyond traditional grammar in a fundamental way, however. As has repeatedly
been emphasized, traditional grammars make an essential appeal to
the intelligence of the reader. They do not actually formulate the rules
of the grammar, but rather give examples and hints that enable the
intelligent reader to determine the grammar, in some way that is not
at all understood. They do not provide an analysis of the 'faculté de
langage' that makes this achievement possible. To carry the study of
language beyond its traditional bounds, it is necessary to recognize
this limitation and to develop means to transcend it. This is the
fundamental problem to which all work in generative grammar has
been addressed.

The most striking aspect of linguistic competence is what we may
call the 'creativity of language', that is, the speaker's ability to produce
new sentences, sentences that are immediately understood by other
speakers although they bear no physical resemblance to sentences
which are 'familiar'. The fundamental importance of this creative
aspect of normal language use has been recognized since the seventeenth century at least, and it was at the core of Humboldtian general
linguistics. Modern linguistics, however, is seriously at fault in its
failure to come to grips with this central problem. In fact, even to
speak of the hearer's 'familiarity with sentences' is an absurdity.
Normal use of language involves the production and interpretation of
sentences that are similar to sentences that have been heard before
only in that they are generated by the rules of the same grammar, and
thus the only sentences that can in any serious sense be called 'familiar'
are clichés or fixed formulas of one sort or another. The extent to
which this is true has been seriously underestimated even by those
linguists (e.g. O. Jespersen) who have given some attention to the
problem of creativity. This is evident from the common description of
language use as a matter of 'grammatical habit' [e.g. O. Jespersen,
Philosophy of grammar (London, 1924)]. It is important to recognize that
there is no sense of 'habit' known to psychology in which this
characterization of language use is true (just as there is no notion of
'generalization' known to psychology or philosophy that entitles us to

characterize the new sentences of ordinary linguistic usage as generalizations of previous performance). The familiarity of the reference to normal
language use as a matter of 'habit' or as based on 'generalization'
in some fundamental way must not blind one to the realization that
these characterizations are simply untrue if terms are used in any
technical or well-defined sense, and that they can be accepted only as
metaphors—highly misleading metaphors, since they tend to lull the
linguist into the entirely erroneous belief that the problem of accounting for the creative aspect of normal language use is not after all a
very serious one.

Returning now to the central topic, a *generative grammar* (that is, an
explicit grammar that makes no appeal to the reader's 'faculté de
langage' but rather attempts to incorporate the mechanisms of this
faculty) is a system of rules that relate signals to semantic interpretations of these signals. It is *descriptively adequate* to the extent that this
pairing corresponds to the competence of the idealized speaker-hearer.
The idealization is (in particular) that in the study of grammar we
abstract away from the many other factors (e.g. memory limitations,
distractions, changes of intention in the course of speaking, etc.) that
interact with underlying competence to produce actual performance.

If a generative grammar is to pair signals with semantic interpretations, then the theory of generative grammar must provide a general,
language-independent means for representing the signals and semantic
interpretations that are interrelated by the grammars of particular
languages. This fact has been recognized since the origins of linguistic
theory, and traditional linguistics made various attempts to develop
theories of universal phonetics and universal semantics that might
meet this requirement. Without going into any detail, I think it would
be widely agreed that the general problem of universal phonetics is
fairly well-understood (and has been, in fact, for several centuries),
whereas the problems of universal semantics still remain veiled in their
traditional obscurity. We have fairly reasonable techniques of phonetic
representation that seem to approach adequacy for all known languages,
though, of course, there is much to learn in this domain. In contrast,
the immediate prospects for universal semantics seem much more dim,
though surely this is no reason for the study to be neglected (quite
the opposite conclusion should, obviously, be drawn). In fact, recent
work of Katz, Fodor, and Postal (see section 5), seems to me to suggest
new and interesting ways to reopen these traditional questions.

The fact that universal semantics is in a highly unsatisfactory state does not imply that we must abandon the programme of constructing grammars that pair signals and semantic interpretations. For although there is little that one can say about the language-independent system of semantic representation, a great deal is known about conditions that semantic representations must meet, in particular cases. Let us then introduce the neutral technical notion of 'syntactic description', and take a syntactic description of a sentence to be an (abstract) object of some sort, associated with the sentence, that uniquely determines its semantic interpretation (the latter notion being left unspecified pending further insights into semantic theory) as well as its phonetic form. A particular linguistic theory must specify the set of possible syntactic descriptions for sentences of a natural language. The extent to which these syntactic descriptions meet the conditions that we know must apply to semantic interpretations provides one measure of the success and sophistication of the grammatical theory in question. As the theory of generative grammar has progressed, the notion of syntactic description has been clarified and extended. I will discuss below some recent ideas on just what should constitute the syntactic description of a sentence, if the theory of generative grammar is to provide descriptively adequate grammars.

Notice that a syntactic description (henceforth, SD) may convey information about a sentence beyond its phonetic form and semantic interpretation. Thus we should expect a descriptively adequate grammar of English to express the fact that the expressions (1)–(3) are ranked in the order given in terms of 'degree of deviation' from English, quite apart from the question of how interpretations can be imposed on them [in the case of (2) and (3)]:

(1)   the dog looks terrifying
(2)   the dog looks barking
(3)   the dog looks lamb

A generative grammar, then, must at least determine a pairing of signals with SD's; and a theory of generative grammar must provide a general characterization of the class of possible signals (a theory of phonetic representation) and the class of possible SD's. A grammar is descriptively adequate to the extent that it is factually correct in a variety of respects, in particular, to the extent that it pairs signals with SD's that do in fact meet empirically given conditions on the semantic interpretations that they support. For example, if a signal has two intrinsic semantic interpretations in a particular language [e.g. (4) or

(5), in English], a grammar of this language will approach descriptive adequacy if it assigns two SD's to the sentence, and, beyond this, it will approach descriptive adequacy to the extent that these SD's succeed in expressing the basis for the ambiguity.

(4)   they don't know how good meat tastes

(5)   what disturbed John was being disregarded by everyone

In the case of (4), for example, a descriptively adequate grammar must not only assign two SD's to the sentence but must also do so in such a way that in one of these the grammatical relations of *good*, *meat*, and *taste* are as in 'meat tastes good', while in the other they are as in 'meat which is good tastes Adjective' (where the notion 'grammatical relation' is to be defined in a general way within the linguistic theory in question), this being the basis for the alternative semantic interpretations that may be assigned to this sentence. Similarly, in the case of (5), it must assign to the pair *disregard-John* the same grammatical relation as in 'everyone disregards John', in one SD; whereas in the other it must assign this very same relation to the pair *disregard-what* (*disturbed John*), and must assign no semantically functional grammatical relation at all to *disregard-John*. On the other hand, in the case of (6) and (7) only one SD should be assigned by a descriptively adequate grammar. This SD should, in the case of (6), indicate that *John* is related to *incompetent* as it is in 'John is incompetent' and, that *John* is related to *regard* (*as incompetent*) as it is in 'everyone regards John as incompetent'. In the case of (7), the SD must indicate that *our* is related to *regard* (*as incompetent*) as *us* is related to *regard* (*as incompetent*) in 'everyone regards us as incompetent'.

(6)   what disturbed John was being regarded
             as incompetent by everyone.

(7)   what disturbed John was our being regarded
             as incompetent by everyone.

Similarly, in the case of (8), the grammar must assign four distinct SD's, each of which specifies the system of grammatical relations that underlies one of the distinct semantic interpretations of this sentence:

(8)   the police were ordered to stop drinking after midnight.

Examples such as these should suffice to illustrate what is involved in the problem of constructing descriptively adequate generative grammars and developing a theory of grammar that analyses and studies in full generality the concepts that appear in these particular grammars. It is quite evident from innumerable examples of this sort that the conditions on semantic interpretations are sufficiently clear and rich so that the problem of defining the notion 'syntactic description' and developing descriptively adequate grammars (relative to this notion of SD) can be made quite concrete, despite the fact that the notion 'semantic interpretation' itself still resists any deep analysis. We return to some recent ideas on semantic interpretation of SD's in section 5.

A grammar, once again, must pair signals and SD's. The SD assigned to a signal must determine the semantic interpretation of the signal, in some way which, in detail, remains unclear. Furthermore, each SD must uniquely determine the signal of which it is the SD (uniquely, that is, up to free variation). Hence the SD must (i) determine a semantic interpretation and (ii) determine a phonetic representation. Let us define the 'deep structure of a sentence' as that aspect of the SD that determines its semantic interpretation, and the 'surface structure of a sentence' as that aspect of the SD that determines its phonetic form. A grammar, then, must consist of three components: a *syntactic component*, which generates SD's, each of which consists of a surface structure and a deep structure; a *semantic component*, which assigns a semantic interpretation to a deep structure; a *phonological component*, which assigns a phonetic interpretation to a surface structure. Thus the grammar as a whole will associate phonetic representations and semantic interpretations, as required, this association being mediated by the syntactic component that generates deep and surface structures as elements of SD's.

The notions 'deep structure' and 'surface structure' are intended as explications of the Humboldtian notions 'inner form of a sentence' and 'outer form of a sentence' (the general notion 'form' is probably more properly to be related to the notion 'generative grammar' itself). The terminology is suggested by the usage familiar in contemporary analytic philosophy [cf. for example, Wittgenstein, *Philosophical Investigations* 168 (Oxford, 1953)]. C. F. Hockett has also used these terms [*A course in modern linguistics*, Ch. 29 (New York, 1958)] in roughly the same sense.

There is good reason to suppose that the surface structure of a sentence is a labelled bracketing that segments it into its continuous constituents, categorizes these, segments the constituents into further categorized constituents, etc. Thus underlying (6), for example, is a surface structure that analyses it into its constituents (perhaps, 'what

disturbed John', 'was', 'being regarded as incompetent by everyone'),
assigning each of these to a certain category indicated by the labelling,
then further segmenting each of these into its constituents (e.g. perhaps,
'what disturbed John' into 'what' and 'disturbed John'), each of these
being assigned to a category indicated by the labelling, etc., until ulti-
mate constituents are reached. Information of this sort is, in fact,
necessary to determine the phonetic representation of this sentence. The
labelled bracketing can be presented in a tree-diagram, or in other
familiar notations*.

It is clear, however, that the deep structure must be quite different
from this surface structure. For one thing, the surface representation in no way expresses the grammatical relations that are, as we
have just observed, crucial for semantic interpretation. Secondly, in
the case of an ambiguous sentence such as, for example, (5), only a
single surface structure may be assigned, but the deep structures must
obviously differ. Such examples as these are sufficient to indicate that
the deep structure underlying a sentence cannot be simply a labelled
bracketing of it. Since there is good evidence that the surface structure
should, in fact, simply be a labelled bracketing, we conclude that deep
structures cannot be identified with surface structures. The inability
of surface structure to indicate semantically significant grammatical
relations (i.e. to serve as deep structure) is one fundamental fact that
motivated the development of transformational generative grammar,
in both its classical and modern varieties.

In summary, a full generative grammar must consist of a syntactic,
semantic, and phonological component. The syntactic component
generates SD's, each of which contains a deep structure and a surface
structure. The semantic component assigns a semantic interpretation
to the deep structure and the phonological component assigns a
phonetic interpretation to the surface structure. An ambiguous

---

* Thus, the sentence 'The noise disturbed John' can be represented as a labelled
bracketing:

$$(((The)^{Det} (noise)^N)^{NP} ((disturbed)^{Vb} (John)^N)^{VP})^S$$

or as a tree-diagram:

sentence has several SD's, differing in the deep structures that they contain (though the converse need not be true).

To go on from here to develop a substantive linguistic theory we must provide:

(9) (i)   theories of phonetic and semantic representation
    (ii) a general account of the notion 'syntactic description'
    (iii) a specification of the class of potential generative grammars
    (iv) a general account of how these grammars function, that is, how they generate SD's and assign to them phonetic and semantic interpretations, thus pairing phonetically represented signals with semantic interpretations.

I have been discussing so far only the question of descriptive adequacy of grammars and the problem of developing a linguistic theory that will provide the basis for the construction of descriptively adequate grammars. As has been repeatedly emphasized, however, the goals of linguistic theory can be set much higher than this; and, in fact, it is a prerequisite even for the study of descriptive adequacy that they be set higher than this. It is essential also to raise the question of 'explanatory adequacy' of linguistic theory. The nature of this question can be appreciated readily in terms of the problem of constructing a hypothetical language-acquisition device AD that can provide as 'output' a descriptively adequate grammer G for the language L on the basis of certain primary linguistic data from L as an input; that is, a device represented schematically as (10):

(10)   primary linguistic data → $\boxed{\text{AD}}$ → G

We naturally want the device AD to be language-independent—that is, capable of learning any human language and only these. We want it, in other words, to provide an implicit definition of the notion 'human language'. Were we able to develop the specifications for a language-acquisition device of this sort, we could realistically claim to be able to provide an explanation for the linguistic intuition—the tacit competence—of the speaker of a language. This explanation would be based on the assumption that the specifications of the device AD provide the basis for language acquisition, primary linguistic data from some language providing the empirical conditions under which the development of a generative grammar takes place. The difficulties of developing an empirically adequate language-independent specification of AD are too obvious to require extended discussion; the vital importance of raising this problem and pursuing it intensively at every stage of linguistic investigation also seems to me entirely beyond the possibility of debate.

To pursue the study of explanatory adequacy, we may proceed in two parallel ways. First, we must attempt to provide as narrow a specification of the aspects of linguistic theory listed in (9) as is compatible with the known diversity of languages—we must, in other words, develop as rich a hypothesis concerning linguistic universals as can be supported by available evidence. This specification can then be attributed to the system AD as an intrinsic property. Second, we may attempt to develop a general evaluation procedure, as an intrinsic property of AD, which will enable it to select a particular member of the class of grammars that meet the specifications (9) (or, conceivably, to select a small set of alternatives, though this abstract possibility is hardly worth discussing for the present) on the basis of the presented primary linguistic data. This procedure will then enable the device to select one of the a priori possible hypotheses—one of the permitted grammars—that is compatible with the empirically given data from a given language. Having selected such a hypothesis, it has 'mastered' the language described by this grammar (and it thus knows a great deal beyond what it has explicitly 'learned'). Given a linguistic theory that specifies (9) and an evaluation procedure, we can explain some aspect of the speaker's competence whenever we can show with some plausibility that this aspect of his competence is determined by the most highly valued grammar of the permitted sort that is compatible with data of the kind to which he has actually been exposed.

Notice that an evaluation procedure (simplicity measure, as it is often called in technical discussion) is itself an empirical hypothesis concerning universal properties of language; it is, in other words, a hypothesis, true or false, about the prerequisites for language-acquisition. To support or refute this hypothesis, we must consider evidence as to the factual relation between primary linguistic data and descriptively adequate grammars. We must ask whether the proposed evaluation procedure in fact can mediate this empirically-given relation. An evaluation procedure, therefore, has much the status of a physical constant; in particular, it is impossible to support or reject a specific proposal on the basis of a priori argument.

It is important to recognize that there is nothing controversial in what has just been said. One may or may not choose to deal with the problem of explanatory adequacy. One who chooses to overlook this problem may (and, in my opinion, surely will) find that he has eliminated from consideration one of the most important sources of evidence bearing on the problems that remain (in particular, the problem of descriptive adequacy)*. His situation, then, may be quite analogous to that of the person who has decided to limit his attention to surface structures (to the exclusion of deep structures) or to first halves of sentences. He must show that the delimitation of interest leaves him with a viable subject. But, in any event, he surely has no basis for objecting to the attempt on the part of other linguists to study the general question of which he has (artificially, in my opinion) delimited one facet.

Topics in the Theory of Generative Grammar (*1966*), *9–17, 18, 20–3*

We have not yet considered the following very crucial question: What is the relation between the general theory and the particular grammars that follow from it? In other words, what sense can we give to the notion 'follow from', in this context? It is at this point that our approach will diverge sharply from many theories of linguistic structure.

The strongest requirement that could be placed on the relation between a theory of linguistic structure and particular grammars is that the theory must provide a practical and mechanical method for actually constructing the grammar, given a corpus of utterances.

* The reason for this is quite simple. Choice of a descriptively adequate grammar for the language L is always much underdetermined (for the linguist, that is) by data from L. Other relevant data can be adduced from study of descriptively adequate grammars of other languages, but only if the linguist has an explanatory theory of the sort just sketched. Such a theory can receive empirical support from its success in providing descriptively adequate grammars for other languages. Furthermore, it prescribes, in advance, the form of the grammar of L and the evaluation procedure that leads to the selection of this grammar, given data. In this way, it permits data from other languages to play a role in justifying the grammar selected as an empirical hypothesis concerning the speakers of L. This approach is quite natural. Following it, the linguist comes to a conclusion about the speakers of L on the basis of an independently supported assumption about the nature of language in general—an assumption, that is, concerning the general 'faculté de langage' that makes language-acquisition possible. The general explanatory theory of language and the specific theory of a particular language that results from application of the general theory to data each has psychological content, the first as a hypothesis about innate mental structure, the second as a hypothesis about the tacit knowledge that emerges with exposure to appropriate experience. [C]

Let us say that such a theory provides us with a *discovery procedure* for grammars.

A weaker requirement would be that the theory must provide a practical and mechanical method for determining whether or not a grammar proposed for a given corpus is, in fact, the best grammar of the language from which this corpus is drawn. Such a theory, which is not concerned with the question of *how* this grammar was constructed, might be said to provide a *decision procedure* for grammars.

An even weaker requirement would be that given a corpus and given two proposed grammars G_1 and G_2, the theory must tell us which is the better grammar of the language from which the corpus is drawn. In this case we might say that the theory provides an *evaluation procedure* for grammars.

The point of view adopted here is that it is unreasonable to demand of linguistic theory that it provide anything more than a practical evaluation procedure for grammars. That is, we adopt the weakest of the three positions described above. As I interpret most of the more careful proposals for the development of linguistic theory, they attempt to meet the strongest of these three requirements. That is, they attempt to state methods of analysis that an investigator might actually use, if he had the time, to construct a grammar of a language directly from the raw data. I think that it is very questionable that this goal is attainable in any interesting way, and I suspect that any attempt to meet it will lead into a maze of more and more elaborate and complex analytic procedures that will fail to provide answers for many important questions about the nature of linguistic structure. I believe that by lowering our sights to the more modest goal of developing an evaluation procedure for grammars we can focus attention more clearly on really crucial problems of linguistic structure and we can arrive at more satisfying answers to them. The correctness of this judgment can only be determined by the actual development and comparison of theories of these various sorts. Notice, however, that the weakest of these three requirements is still strong enough to guarantee significance for a theory that meets it. There are few areas of science in which one would seriously consider the possibility of developing a general, practical, mechanical method for choosing among several theories, each compatible with the available data.

Syntactic Structures, 50–3

1.3 *The independence of grammar*

From now on I will consider a *language* to be a set (finite or infinite) of sentences, each finite in length and constructed out of a finite set of elements. All natural languages in their spoken or written form are languages in this sense, since each natural language has a finite number of phonemes (or letters in its alphabet) and each sentence is representable as a finite sequence of these phonemes (or letters), though there are infinitely many sentences. Similarly, the set of 'sentences' of some formalized system of mathematics can be considered a language. The fundamental aim in the linguistic analysis of a language L is to separate the *grammatical* sequences which are the sentences of L from the *ungrammatical* sequences which are not sentences of L and to study the structure of the grammatical sequences. The grammar of L will thus be a device that generates all of the grammatical sequences of L and none of the ungrammatical ones. One way to test the adequacy of a grammar proposed for L is to determine whether or not the sequences that it generates are actually grammatical, i.e. acceptable to a native speaker, etc. We can take certain steps towards providing a behavioral criterion for grammaticalness so that this test of adequacy can be carried out. For the purposes of this discussion, however, suppose that we assume intuitive knowledge of the grammatical sentences of English and ask what sort of grammar will be able to do the job of producing these in some effective and illuminating way. We thus face a familiar task of explication of some intuitive concept—in this case, the concept 'grammatical in English', and more generally, the concept 'grammatical'.

Notice that in order to set the aims of grammar significantly it is sufficient to assume a partial knowledge of sentences and non-sentences. That is, we may assume for this discussion that certain sequences of phonemes are definitely sentences, and that certain other sequences are definitely non-sentences. In many intermediate cases we shall be prepared to let the grammar itself decide, when the grammar is set up in the simplest way so that it includes the clear sentences and excludes the clear non-sentences. This is a familiar feature of explication. A certain number of clear cases, then, will provide us with a criterion of adequacy for any particular grammar. For a single language, taken in isolation, this provides only a weak test of adequacy, since many different grammars may handle the clear cases properly. This can be generalized to a very strong condition, however, if we insist that the clear cases be handled properly for *each* language by grammars, all of which are constructed by the same method. That is, each grammar is related to the corpus of sentences in the language it describes in a way fixed in advance for all grammars by a given linguistic theory. We then have a very strong test of adequacy for a linguistic theory that attempts to give a general explanation for the notion 'grammatical sentence' in terms of 'observed sentence', and for the set of grammars constructed in accordance with such a theory. It is furthermore a reasonable requirement, since we are interested not only in particular languages, but also in the general nature of Language. There is a great deal more that can be said about this crucial topic, but this would take us too far afield.

On what basis do we actually go about separating grammatical sequences from ungrammatical sequences? I shall not attempt to give a complete answer to this question here, but I would like to point out that several answers that immediately suggest themselves could not be correct. First, it is obvious that the set of grammatical sentences cannot be identified with any particular corpus of utterances obtained by the linguist in his field work. Any grammar of a language will *project* the finite and somewhat accidental corpus of observed utterances to a set (presumably infinite) of grammatical utterances. In this respect, a grammar mirrors the behaviour of the speaker who, on the basis of a finite and accidental experience with language, can produce or understand an indefinite number of new sentences. Indeed, any explication of the notion 'grammatical in L' (i.e. any characterization of 'grammatical in L' in terms of 'observed utterance of L') can be thought of as offering an explanation for this fundamental aspect of linguistic behaviour.

Second, the notion 'grammatical' cannot be identified with 'meaningful' or 'significant' in any semantic sense. Sentences (11) and (12) are equally nonsensical, but any speaker of English will recognize that only the former is grammatical.

(11)   Colourless green ideas sleep furiously.
(12)   Furiously sleep ideas green colourless.

Similarly, there is no semantic reason to prefer (13) to (15) or (14) to (16), but only (13) and (14) are grammatical sentences of English.

(13)   have you a book on modern music?
(14)   the book seems interesting.
(15)   read you a book on modern music?
(16)   the child seems sleeping.

Such examples suggest that any search for a semantically based definition of 'grammaticalness' will be futile. We shall see, in fact, that there are deep structural reasons for distinguishing (13) and (14) from (15) and (16); but before we are able to find an explanation for such facts as these we shall have to carry the theory of syntactic structure a good deal beyond its familiar limits.

Third, the notion 'grammatical in English' cannot be identified in any way with the notion 'high order of statistical approximation to English'. It is fair to assume that neither sentence (11) nor (12) (nor indeed any part of these sentences) has ever occurred in an English discourse. Hence, in any statistical model for grammaticalness, these sentences will be ruled out on identical grounds as equally 'remote' from English. Yet (11), though nonsensical, is grammatical, while (12) is not. Presented with these sentences, a speaker of English will read (11) with a normal sentence intonation, but he will read (12) with a falling intonation on each word; in fact, with just the intonation pattern given to any sequence of unrelated words. He treats each word in (12) as a separate phrase. Similarly, he will be able to recall (11) much more easily than (12), to learn it much more quickly, etc. Yet he may never have heard or seen any pair of words from these sentences joined in actual discourse. To choose another example, in the context 'I saw a fragile —', the words 'whale' and 'of' may have equal (i.e. zero) frequency in the past linguistic experience of a speaker who will immediately recognize that one of these substitutions, but not the other, gives a grammatical sentence. We cannot of course, appeal to the fact that sentences such as (11) 'might' be uttered in some sufficiently far-fetched context, while (12) would never be, since the basis for this differentiation between (11) and (12) is precisely what we are interested in determining.

Evidently, one's ability to produce and recognize grammatical utterances is not based on notions of statistical approximation and the like. The custom of calling grammatical sentences those that 'can occur', or those that are 'possible', has been responsible for some confusion here. It is natural to understand 'possible' as meaning 'highly probable' and to assume that the linguist's sharp distinction between grammatical and ungrammatical* is motivated by a feeling

---

* In section 5.4 we shall suggest that this sharp distinction may be modified in favour of a notion of levels of grammaticalness. But this has no bearing on the point at issue here. Thus (11) and (12) will be at different levels of grammaticalness even if (11) is assigned a lower degree of grammaticalness than, say, (13) and (14); but they will

that since the 'reality' of language is too complex to be described completely, he must content himself with a schematized version replacing 'zero probability, and all extremely low probabilities, by *impossible*, and all higher probabilities by *possible*'*. We see, however, that this idea is quite incorrect, and that a structural analysis cannot be understood as a schematic summary developed by sharpening the blurred edges in the full statistical picture. If we rank the sequences of a given length in order of statistical approximation to English, we will find both grammatical and ungrammatical sequences scattered throughout the list; there appears to be no particular relation between order of approximation and grammaticalness. Despite the undeniable interest and importance of semantic and statistical studies of language, they appear to have no direct relevance to the problem of determining or characterizing the set of grammatical utterances. I think that we are forced to conclude that grammar is autonomous and independent of meaning, and that probabilistic models give no particular insight into some of the basic problems of syntactic structure.

Syntactic Structures, 13–17

---

be at the same level of statistical remoteness from English. The same is true of an indefinite number of similar pairs. [C]

* C. F. Hockett, *A manual of phonology* (Baltimore, 1955), p. 10.

2 Syntax: I

(*SYNTACTIC STRUCTURES*, *1957*)

2.1 *Introductory*

One way of providing a finite representation of the morphemic structure of English sentences is by means of a machine called a 'finite state grammar'. A finite state grammar can be represented graphically in the form of a 'state diagram'. For example, the grammar that produces just the two sentences 'the man comes' and 'the men come' can be represented by the following state diagram:

(1)

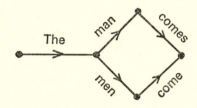

We can extend this grammar to produce an infinite number of sentences by adding closed loops. Thus the finite state grammar of the sub-part of English containing the above sentences in addition to 'the old man comes', 'the old old man comes', . . ., 'the old men come', 'the old old men come', . . ., can be represented by the following state diagram:

(2)

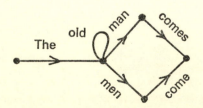

Given a state diagram, we produce a sentence by tracing a path from the initial point on the left to the final point on the right, always proceeding in the direction of the arrows. Having reached a certain point in the diagram, we can proceed along any path leading from this point, whether or not this path has been traversed before in constructing the sentence in question. Each node in such a diagram thus corresponds to a state of the machine. We can allow transition from one state to another in several ways, and we can have any number of closed loops of any length.

If we adopt this conception of language, we can view the speaker as being essentially a machine of the type considered. In producing a sentence, the speaker begins in the initial state, produces the first word of the sentence, thereby switching into a second state which limits the choice of the second word, etc. Each state through which he passes represents the grammatical restrictions that limit the choice of the next word at this point in the utterance.

However, it is well known that English contains structures of the following types:

(3)   (i) If S_1, then S_2.
      (ii) Either S_3, or S_4.
      (iii) The man who said that S_5, is arriving today.

In each of the above structures there is a dependency relation between words on opposite sides of the comma (i.e. 'if'—'then', 'either'—'or', 'man'—'is'), and we can insert a declarative sentence S_1, S_3, S_5 between the interdependent words. We cannot make the correct selection of 'then', 'or', 'is' without being able to refer back to the previous words 'if', 'either', 'man'. It can be shown that the set of all such sentences cannot be described by a finite state grammar. It follows that the speaker's knowledge of English cannot be represented by a system of states that produces sentences from left to right, passing through successive states and emitting an element with each interstate transition. If this limited linguistic theory is not adequate we are forced to search for some more powerful type of grammar and some more 'abstract' form of linguistic theory. A central notion in linguistic theory has been that of 'linguistic level'. According to this concept, language structure consists of a finite set of 'levels of representation', ordered from high to low, and so constructed that we can state all the permitted sequences of elements at each level, and the constituency of each higher level element in terms of elements of the level next below.

During the course of our inquiry we shall be obliged to give up the notion of a finite set of levels of representation.

Syntactic Structures, 18–25, summarized

2.2 *Phrase structure grammar*

Customarily, linguistic description on the syntactic level is formulated in terms of constituent analysis (parsing). We now ask what form of grammar is presupposed by description of this sort. We find that the new form of grammar is *essentially* more powerful than the finite state model rejected above, and that the associated concept of 'linguistic level' is different in fundamental respects.

As a simple example of the new form for grammars associated with constituent analysis, consider the following:

(4) (i) *Sentence→NP+VP*
    (ii) *NP→T+N*
    (iii) *VP→Verb+NP*
    (iv) *T→the*
    (v) *N→man, ball,* etc.
    (vi) *Verb→hit, took,* etc.

Suppose that we interpret each rule $X→Y$ of (4) as the instruction 'rewrite X as Y'. We shall call (5) a *derivation* of the sentence 'the man hit the ball', where the numbers at the right of each line of the derivation refer to the rule of the 'grammar' (4) used in constructing that line from the preceding line.

(5) *Sentence*
    NP+VP   (i)
    T+N+VP   (ii)
    T+N+Verb+NP   (iii)
    the+N+Verb+NP   (iv)
    the+man+Verb+NP   (v)
    the+man+hit+NP   (vi)
    the+man+hit+T+N   (ii)
    the+man+hit+the+N   (iv)
    the+man+hit+the+ball   (v)

Thus the second line of (5) is formed from the first line by rewriting *Sentence* as *NP+VP* in accordance with rule (i) of (4); the third line is formed from the second by rewriting *NP* as *T+N* in accordance with rule (ii) of (4); etc. We can represent the derivation (5) in an obvious way by means of the following tree diagram*:

(6)

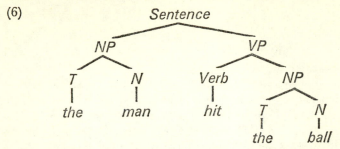

The diagram (6) conveys less information than the derivation (5), since it does not tell us in what order the rules were applied in (5). Given (5), we can construct (6) uniquely, but not vice versa, since it is possible to construct a derivation that reduces to (6) with a different order of application of the rules. The diagram (6) retains just what is essential in (5) for the determination of the phrase structure (constituent analysis) of the derived sentence 'the man hit the ball'. A sequence of words of this sentence is a constituent of type Z if we can trace this sequence back to a single point of origin in (6), and this point of origin is labelled Z. Thus 'hit the ball' can be traced back to VP in (6); hence 'hit the ball' is a VP in the derived sentence. But 'man hit' cannot be traced back to any single point of origin in (6); hence 'man hit' is not a constituent at all.

We say that two derivations are *equivalent* if they reduce to the same diagram of the form (6). Occasionally, a grammar may permit us to construct nonequivalent derivations for a given sentence. Under these circumstances, we say that we have a case of 'constructional homonymity', and if our grammar is correct, this sentence of the language should be ambiguous.

One generalization of (4) is clearly necessary. We must be able to limit application of a rule to a certain context. Thus T can be rewritten *a* if the following noun is singular, but not if it is plural; similarly, *Verb* can be rewritten 'hits' if the preceding noun is *man*, but not if it is *men*. In general, if we wish to limit the rewriting of X as Y to the context $Z–W$, we can state in the grammar the rule

(7) $Z+X+W \rightarrow Z+Y+W$.

* Otherwise known as a Phrase-marker. [A, B]

For example, in the case of singular and plural verbs, instead of having
$Verb \rightarrow hits$ as an additional rule of (4), we should have

(8) $NP_{sing} + Verb \rightarrow NP_{sing} + hits$

indicating that *Verb* is rewritten *hits* only in the context $NP_{sing}-$.
Correspondingly, (4ii) will have to be restated to include NP_{sing} and
NP_{pl}*. This is a straightforward generalization of (4). One feature
of (4) must be preserved, however, as it is in (8): only a single element
can be rewritten in any single rule; i.e. in (7), X must be a single
symbol such as T, *Verb*, and not a sequence such as $T+N$. If this
condition is not met, we will not be able to recover properly the phrase
structure of derived sentences from the associated diagrams of the
form (6), as we did above.

We can now describe more generally the form of grammar associated
with the theory of linguistic structure based upon constituent analysis.
Each such grammar is defined by a finite set Σ of initial strings and a
finite set F of 'instruction formulas' of the form $X \rightarrow Y$ interpreted:
'rewrite X as Y'. Though X need not be a single symbol, only a single
symbol of X can be rewritten in forming Y. In the grammar (4), the
only member of the set Σ of initial strings was the single symbol
Sentence, and F consisted of the rules (i)–(vi); but we might want to
extend Σ to include, for example, *Declarative Sentence, Interrogative
Sentence*, as additional symbols. Given the grammar [Σ, F], we define
a *derivation* as a finite sequence of strings, beginning with an initial
string of Σ, and with each string in the sequence being derived from the
preceding string by application of one of the instruction formulas of
F. Thus (5) is a derivation, and the five-termed sequence of strings
consisting of the first five lines of (5) is also a derivation. Certain
derivations are *terminated* derivations, in the sense that their final
string cannot be rewritten any further by the rules F. Thus (5) is a

---

* Thus in a more complete grammar, (4ii) might be replaced by a set of rules that
includes the following:

$$NP \rightarrow \left\{ \begin{matrix} NP_{sing} \\ NP_{pl} \end{matrix} \right\}$$
$$NP_{sing} \rightarrow T+N+\emptyset(+ \text{ Prepositional Phrase})$$
$$NP_{pl} \rightarrow T+N+S \ (+ \text{ Prepositional Phrase})$$

where S is the morpheme which is singular for verbs and plural for nouns ('comes',
'boys'), and $\emptyset$ is the morpheme which is singular for nouns and plural for verbs
('boy', 'come'). We shall omit all mention of first and second person throughout
this discussion. Identification of the nominal and verbal number affix is actually of
questionable validity. [C]

terminated derivation, but the sequence consisting of the first five lines of (5) is not. If a string is the last line of a terminated derivation, we say that it is a *terminal* string. Thus *the+man+hit+the+ball* is a terminal string from the grammar (4). Some grammars of the form [Σ, F] may have no terminal strings, but we are interested only in grammars that do have terminal strings, i.e. that describe some language. A set of strings is called a *terminal language* if it is the set of terminal strings for some grammar [Σ, F]. Thus each such grammar defines some terminal language (perhaps the 'empty' language containing no sentences), and each terminal language is produced by some grammar of the form [Σ, F]. Given a terminal language and its grammar, we can reconstruct the phrase structure of each sentence of the language (each terminal string of the grammar) by considering the associated diagrams of the form (6), as we saw above. We can also define the grammatical relations in these languages in a formal way in terms of the associated diagrams.

Suppose that by a [Σ, F] grammar we can generate all of the grammatical sequences of morphemes of a language. In order to complete the grammar we must state the phonemic structure of these morphemes, so that the grammar will produce the grammatical phoneme sequences of the language. But this statement (which we would call the *morphophonemics* of the language) can also be given by a set of rules of the form 'rewrite X as Y', e.g. for English:

(9)   (i)   *walk*→/wɔk/
      (ii) *take+past*→/tuk/
      (iii) *hit+past*→/hit/
      (iv) ...D/+*past*→/...D/+/ɪd/ (where D = /t/ or /d/)
      (v)   /...C_{unv}/+*past*→/...C_{unv}/+/t/ (where C_{unv} is an unvoiced consonant)
      (vi) *past*→/d/
      (vii) *take*→/teyk/
            etc.

or something similar. Note, incidentally, that order must be defined among these rules—e.g. (ii) must precede (v) or (vii), or we will derive such forms as /teykt/ for the past tense of *take*. In these morphophonemic rules we need no longer require that only a single symbol be rewritten in each rule.

We can now extend the phrase structure derivations by applying (9), so that we have a unified process for generating phoneme sequences from the initial string *Sentence*. This makes it appear as though the break between the higher level of phrase structure and the lower levels is arbitrary. Actually, the distinction is not arbitrary. For one thing, as we have seen, the formal properties of the rules $X \rightarrow Y$ corresponding to phrase structure are different from those of the morphophonemic rules, since in the case of the former we must require that only a single symbol be rewritten. Second, the elements that figure in the rules (9) can be classified into a finite set of levels (e.g. phonemes and morphemes; or, perhaps, phonemes, morphophonemes, and morphemes) each of which is elementary in the sense that a single string of elements of this level is associated with each sentence as its representation on this level (except in cases of homonymity), and each such string represents a single sentence. But the elements that appear in the rules corresponding to phrase structure cannot be classified into higher and lower levels in this way. We shall see below that there is an even more fundamental reason for marking this subdivision into the higher level rules of phrase structure and the lower level rules that convert strings of morphemes into strings of phonemes.

Syntactic Structures, 26–30, 32–3

2.3 *Limitations of phrase structure grammar*

[We have seen that a phrase structure grammar based on immediate constituent analysis is more powerful than a model based on a finite state process, and does not fail in the same way. However, a phrase structure grammar also has serious shortcomings. As soon as we consider any sentences beyond the simplest type, and in particular, when we attempt to define some order among the rules that produce these sentences, we find that we run into numerous difficulties and complications. Here we shall limit ourselves to sketching a few simple cases in which considerable improvement is possible over grammars of the form [Σ, F].]

One of the most productive processes for forming new sentences is the process of conjunction. If we have two sentences $Z+X+W$ and $Z+Y+W$, and if X and Y are actually constituents of these sentences, we can generally form a new sentence $Z–X+and+Y–W$. For example, from the sentences (10a–b) we can form the new sentence (11).

(10)   (a) the scene—of the movie—was in Chicago
         (b) the scene—of the play—was in Chicago
(11)   the scene—of the movie and of the play—was in Chicago.

If X and Y are, however, not constituents, we generally cannot do this. For example we cannot form (13) from (12a–b).

(12)   (a) the—liner sailed down the—river
       (b) the—tugboat chugged up the—river
(13)   the—liner sailed down and the tugboat chugged up the—river.

Similarly, if X and Y are both constituents, but are constituents of different kinds (i.e. if in the diagram of the form (6) they each have a single origin, but this origin is labelled differently), then we cannot in general form a new sentence by conjunction. For example, we cannot form (15) from (14a–b).

(14)   (a) the scene—of the movie—was in Chicago
       (b) the scene—that I wrote—was in Chicago
(15)   the scene—of the movie and that I wrote—was in Chicago.

In fact, the possibility of conjunction offers one of the best criteria for the initial determination of phrase structure. We can simplify the description of conjunction if we try to set up constituents in such a way that the following rule will hold:

(16)   If S_1 and S_2 are grammatical sentences, and S_1 differs from S_2
       only in that X appears in S_1 where Y appears in S_2 (i.e. $S_1 =$
       $..X..$ and $S_2 = ..Y..$), and X and Y are constituents of the
       same type in S_1 and S_2, respectively, then S_3 is a sentence, where
       S_3 is the result of replacing X by $X+and+Y$ in S_1 (i.e. $S_3 =$
       $..X+and+Y..$).

Even though additional qualification is necessary here, the grammar is enormously simplified if we set up constituents in such a way that (16) holds even approximately. That is, it is easier to state the distribution of 'and' by means of qualifications on this rule than to do so directly without such a rule. But we now face the following difficulty: we cannot incorporate the rule (16) or anything like it in a grammar $[\Sigma, F]$ of phrase structure, because of certain fundamental limitations on such grammars. The essential property of rule (16) is that in order to apply it to sentences S_1 and S_2 to form the new sentence S_3 we must know not only the actual form of S_1 and S_2 but also their constituent structure—we must know not only the final shape of these sentences, but also their 'history of derivation'. But each rule $X \rightarrow Y$ of the grammar $[\Sigma, F]$ applies or fails to apply to a given string by virtue of the actual substance of this string. The question of how this string gradually assumed this form is irrelevant. If the string contains X as a substring, the rule $X \rightarrow Y$ can apply to it; if not, the rule cannot apply.

We can put this somewhat differently. The grammar $[\Sigma, F]$ can also be regarded as a very elementary process that generates sentences not from 'left to right' but from 'top to bottom'. Suppose that we have the following grammar of phrase structure:

(17) Σ: *Sentence*
     F: $X_1 \rightarrow Y_1$
        $\vdots$
      $X_n \rightarrow Y_n$

Then we can represent this grammar as a machine with a finite number of internal states, including an initial and a final state. In its initial state it can produce only the element *Sentence*, thereby moving into a new state. It can then produce any string Y_i such that *Sentence* $\rightarrow Y_i$ is one of the rules of F in (17), again moving into a new state. Suppose that Y_i is the string $\ldots X_j \ldots$ Then the machine can produce the string $\ldots Y_j \ldots$ by 'applying' the rule $X_j \rightarrow Y_j$. The machine proceeds in this way from state to state until it finally produces a terminal string; it is now in the final state. The machine thus produces derivations, in the sense of p. 24. The important point is that the state of the machine is completely determined by the string it has just produced (i.e. by the last step of the derivation); more specifically, the state is determined by the subset of 'left-hand' elements X_i of F which are contained in this last-produced string. But rule (16) requires a more powerful machine, which can 'look back' to earlier strings in the derivation in order to determine how to produce the next step in the derivation.

Rule (16) is also fundamentally new in a different sense. It makes essential reference to two distinct sentences S_1 and S_2, but in grammars of the $[\Sigma, F]$ type, there is no way to incorporate such double reference. The fact that rule (16) cannot be incorporated into the grammar of phrase structure indicates that even if this form for grammar is not literally inapplicable to English, it is certainly inadequate in the weaker but sufficient sense considered above. This rule leads to a considerable simplification of the grammar; in fact, it provides one of the best criteria for determining how to set up constituents. We shall see that there are many other rules of the same general type as (16) which play the same dual role.

In the grammar (4) we gave only one way of analysing the element

Verb, namely, as *hit* (cf. 4vi). But even with the verbal root fixed (let us say, as *take*), there are many other forms that this element can assume, e.g. *takes, has+taken, will+take, has+been+taken, is+being+taken*, etc. The study of these 'auxiliary verbs' turns out to be quite crucial in the development of English grammar. We shall see that their behaviour is very regular and simply describable when observed from a point of view that is quite different from that developed above, though it appears to be quite complex if we attempt to incorporate these phrases directly into a [Σ, F] grammar.

Consider first the auxiliaries that appear unstressed; for example, 'has' in 'John has read the book', but not *'does'* in 'John *does* read books'. We can state the occurrence of these auxiliaries in declarative sentences by adding to the grammar (4) the following rules:

(18) (i)   *Verb→Aux+V*

  (ii) *V→hit, take, walk, read*, etc.

  (iii) *Aux→C(M) (have+en) (be+ing) (be+en)*

  (iv) *M→will, can, may, shall, must*

(19)

  (i) $C\rightarrow \begin{cases} S \text{ in the context } \mathcal{NP}_{sing} \\ \varnothing \text{ in the context } \mathcal{NP}_{pl} \\ past \end{cases}$ *

  (ii) Let *Af* stand for any of the affixes *past, S, Ø, en, ing*. Let *v* stand for any *M* or *V*, or *have* or *be* (i.e. for any non-affix in the phrase *Verb*). Then:
  $$Af+v\rightarrow v+Af\#,$$
  where # is interpreted as word boundary.

  (iii) Replace + by # except in the context *v–Af*. Insert # initially and finally.

The interpretation of the notations in (18iii) is as follows: we must choose the element *C*, and we may choose zero or more of the parenthesized elements in the given order. In (19i) we may develop *C* into any of three morphemes, observing the contextual restrictions given. As an example of the application of these rules, we construct a derivation in the style of (5), omitting the initial steps.

(20) *the+man+Verb+the+book*   from (4i–v)

  the+man+Aux+V+the+book   (18i)

  the+man+Aux+read+the+book   (18ii)

---

* We assume here that (4ii) has been extended in the manner of p. 26 (footnote), or something similar. [C]

$the + man + C + have + en + be + ing + read + the + book$

(18iii)—we select the
elements C, $have + en$
and $be + ing$.

$the + man + S + have + en + be + ing + read + the + book$

(19i)

$the + man + have + S \, \# be + en \, \# read + ing \, \# the + book$

(19ii)—three times.

$\# the \, \# man \, \# have + S \, \# be + en \, \# read + ing \, \# the \, \# book \, \#$

(19ii)

The morphophonemic rules (9), etc., will convert the last line of this derivation into:

(21)   the man has been reading the book

in phonemic transcription. Similarly, every other auxiliary verb phrase can be generated (although in fact further restrictions must be placed on these rules so that only grammatical sequences can be generated). Note, incidentally, that the morphophonemic rules will have to include such rules as: $will + S \rightarrow will$, $will + past \rightarrow would$. These rules can be dropped if we rewrite (18iii) so that either C or M, but not both, can be selected. But now the forms *would, could, might, should* must be added to (18iv), and certain 'sequence of tense' statements become more complex. It is immaterial to our further discussion which of these alternative analyses is adopted. Several other minor revisions are possible.

Notice that in order to apply (19i) in (20) we had to use the fact that $the + man$ is a singular noun phrase NP_{sing}. That is, we had to refer back to some earlier step in the derivation in order to determine the constituent structure of $the + man$. (The alternative of ordering (19i) and the rule that develops NP_{sing} into $the + man$ in such a way that (19i) must precede the latter is not possible, for a variety of reasons, some of which appear below, p. 36.) Hence (19i), just like (16), goes beyond the elementary finite state character of grammars of phrase structure, and cannot be incorporated within the $[\Sigma, F]$ grammar.

Rule (19ii) violates the requirements of $[\Sigma, F]$ grammars even more severely. It also requires reference to constituent structure (i.e. past history of derivation) and in addition, we have no way to express the required inversion within the terms of phrase structure. Note that this rule is useful elsewhere in the grammar, at least in the case where *Af* is *ing*. Thus the morphemes *to* and *ing* play a very similar role within the noun phrase in that they convert verb phrases into noun phrases, giving, e.g.

(22) $\left\{ \begin{array}{l} \text{to prove that theorem} \\ \text{proving that theorem} \end{array} \right\}$ was difficult

etc. We can exploit this parallel by adding to the grammar (4) the rule

(23) $NP \rightarrow \left\{ \begin{array}{l} ing \\ to \end{array} \right\} VP$

The rule (19ii) will then convert *ing+prove+that+theorem* into *proving # that+theorem*. A more detailed analysis of the *VP* shows that this parallel extends much further than this, in fact.

The reader can easily determine that to duplicate the effect of (18iii) and (19) without going beyond the bounds of a system [Σ, F] of phrase structure, it would be necessary to give a fairly complex statement. Once again, as in the case of conjunction, we see that significant simplification of the grammar is possible if we are permitted to formulate rules of a more complex type than those that correspond to a system of immediate constituent analysis. By allowing ourselves the freedom of (19ii) we have been able to state the constituency of the auxiliary phrase in (18iii) without regard to the interdependence of its elements, and it is always easier to describe a sequence of independent elements than a sequence of mutually dependent ones. To put the same thing differently, in the auxiliary verb phrase we really have discontinuous elements—e.g. in (20), the elements *have . . en* and *be . .ing*. But discontinuities cannot be handled within [Σ, F] grammars*. In (18iii) we treated these elements as continuous, and we introduced

---

* We might attempt to extend the notions of phrase structure to account for discontinuities. Similarly, one might seek to remedy some of the other deficiencies of Σ, F] grammars by a more complex account of phrase structure. I think that such an approach is ill-advised, and that it can only lead to the development of *ad hoc* and fruitless elaborations. It appears to be the case that the notions of phrase structure are quite adequate for a small part of the language and that the rest of the language can be derived by repeated application of a rather simple set of transformations to the strings given by the phrase structure grammar. If we were to attempt to extend phrase structure grammar to cover the entire language directly, we would lose the simplicity of the limited phrase structure grammar and of the transformational development. This approach would miss the main point of level construction, namely, to rebuild the vast complexity of the actual language more elegantly and systematically by extracting the contribution to this complexity of several linguistic levels, each of which is simple in itself. [C]

the discontinuity by the very simple additional rule (19ii). This analysis of the element *Verb* serves as the basis for a far-reaching and extremely simple analysis of several important features of English syntax.

As a third example of the inadequacy of the conceptions of phrase structure, consider the case of the active-passive relation. Passive sentences are formed by selecting the element *be+en* in rule (18iii). But there are heavy restrictions on this element that make it unique among the elements of the auxiliary phrase. For one thing, *be+en* can be selected only if the following *V* is transitive (e.g. *was+eaten* is permitted, but not *was+occurred*); but with a few exceptions the other elements of the auxiliary phrase can occur freely with verbs. Furthermore, *be+en* cannot be selected if the verb *V* is followed by a noun phrase, as in (20) (e.g. we cannot in general have $NP+is+V+en+NP$, even when *V* is transitive—we cannot have 'lunch is eaten John'). Furthermore, if *V* is transitive and is followed by the prepositional phrase *by+NP*, then we *must* select *be+en* (we can have 'lunch is eaten by John' but not 'John is eating by lunch', etc.). Finally, note that in elaborating (4) into a full-fledged grammar we will have to place many restrictions on the choice of *V* in terms of subject and object in order to permit such sentences as: 'John admires sincerity', 'sincerity frightens John', 'John plays golf', 'John drinks wine', while excluding the 'inverse' non-sentences 'sincerity admires John', 'John frightens sincerity', 'golf plays John', 'wine drinks John'. But this whole network of restrictions fails completely when we choose *be+en* as part of the auxiliary verb. In fact, in this case the same selectional dependencies hold, but in the opposite order. That is, for every sentence $NP_1–V–NP_2$ we can have a corresponding sentence $NP_2–is+Ven–by+NP_1$. If we try to include passives directly in the grammar (4), we shall have to restate all of these restrictions in the opposite order for the case in which *be+en* is chosen as part of the auxiliary verb. This inelegant duplication, as well as the special restrictions involving the element *be+en*, can be avoided only if we deliberately exclude passives from the grammar of phrase structure, and reintroduce them by a rule such as:

(24)   If S_1 is a grammatical sentence of the form

$$NP_1–Aux–V–NP_2,$$

then the corresponding string of the form

$$NP_2–Aux+be+en–V–by+NP_1$$

is also a grammatical sentence.

For example, if *John—C—admire—sincerity* is a sentence, then *sincerity—C+be+en—admire—by+John* (which by (19) and (9) becomes 'sincerity is admired by John') is also a sentence.

We can now drop the element *be+en*, and all of the special restrictions associated with it, from (18iii). The fact that *be+en* requires a transitive verb, that it cannot occur before $V+NP$, that it must occur before $V+by+NP$ (where V is transitive), that it inverts the order of the surrounding noun phrases, is in each case an automatic consequence of rule (24). This rule thus leads to a considerable simplification of the grammar. But (24) is well beyond the limits of $[\Sigma, F]$ grammars. Like (19ii), it requires reference to the constituent structure of the string to which it applies and it carries out an inversion on this string in a structurally determined manner.

2.4 *Transformational rules*

We have discussed three rules ((16), (19), (24)) which materially simplify the description of English but which cannot be incorporated into a $[\Sigma, F]$ grammar. There are a great many other rules of this type, a few of which we shall discuss below. By further study of the limitations of phrase structure grammars with respect to English we can show quite conclusively that these grammars will be so hopelessly complex that they will be without interest unless we incorporate such rules.

If we examine carefully the implications of these supplementary rules, however, we see that they lead to an entirely new conception of linguistic structure. Let us call each such rule a 'grammatical transformation'. A grammatical transformation T operates on a given string (or, as in the case of (16), on a set of strings) with a given constituent structure and converts it into a new string with a new derived constituent structure. To show exactly *how* this operation is performed requires a rather elaborate study which would go far beyond the scope of these remarks, but we can in fact develop a certain fairly complex but reasonably natural algebra of transformations having the properties that we apparently require for grammatical description.

From these few examples we can already detect some of the essential properties of a transformational grammar. For one thing, it is clear that we must define an order of application on these transformations. The passive transformation (24), for example, must apply *before* (19). It must precede (19i), in particular, so that the verbal element in the resulting sentence will have the same number as the new grammatical subject of the passive sentence. And it must precede (19ii) so that the latter rule will apply properly to the new inserted element $be+en$. (In discussing the question of whether or not (19i) can be fitted into a $[\Sigma, F]$ grammar, we mentioned that this rule could not be required to apply before the rule analysing NP_{sing} into $the+man$, etc. One reason for this is now obvious—(19i) must apply after (24), but (24) must apply after the analysis of NP_{sing}, or we will not have the proper selectional relations between the subject and verb and the verb and 'agent' in the passive.)

Secondly, note that certain transformations are *obligatory*, whereas others are only *optional*. For example, (19) must be applied to every derivation, or the result will simply not be a sentence*. But (24), the passive transformation, may or may not be applied in any particular case. Either way the result is a sentence. Hence (19) is an obligatory transformation and (24) is an optional transformation.

This distinction between obligatory and optional transformations leads us to set up a fundamental distinction among the sentences of the language. Suppose that we have a grammar G with a $[\Sigma, F]$ part and a transformational part, and suppose that the transformational part has certain obligatory transformations and certain optional ones. Then we define the *kernel* of the language (in terms of the grammar G) as the set of sentences that are produced when we apply obligatory transformations to the terminal strings of the $[\Sigma, F]$ grammar. The transformational part of the grammar will be set up in such a way that transformations can apply to kernel sentences (more correctly, to the forms that underlie kernel sentences—i.e. to terminal strings of the $[\Sigma, F]$ part of the grammar) or to prior transforms. Thus every sentence of the language will either belong to the kernel or will be derived from the strings underlying one or more kernel sentences by a sequence of one or more transformations.

From these considerations we are led to a picture of grammars as possessing a natural tripartite arrangement. Corresponding to the level of phrase structure, a grammar has a sequence of rules of the form $X \rightarrow Y$, and corresponding to lower levels it has a sequence of morphophonemic rules of the same basic form. Linking these two

---

* But of the three parts of (19i), only the third is obligatory. That is, *past* may occur after NP_{sing} or NP_{pl}. Whenever we have an element such as C in (19i) which must be developed, but perhaps in several alternative ways, we can order the alternatives and make each one but the last optional, and the last, obligatory. [C]

sequences, it has a sequence of transformational rules. Thus the grammar will look something like this:

(25) Σ: *Sentence:*

$$
\begin{aligned}
\text{F:} \quad & \left.\begin{array}{l} X_1 \rightarrow Y_1 \\ \quad : \\ X_n \rightarrow Y_n \end{array}\right\} \text{Phrase structure} \\[1em]
& \left.\begin{array}{l} T_1 \\ \quad : \\ T_j \end{array}\right\} \text{Transformational structure} \\[1em]
& \left.\begin{array}{l} Z_1 \rightarrow W_1 \\ \quad : \\ Z_m \rightarrow W_m \end{array}\right\} \text{Morphophonemics}
\end{aligned}
$$

To produce a sentence from such a grammar we construct an extended derivation beginning with *Sentence*. Running through the rules of F we construct a terminal string that will be a sequence of morphemes, though not necessarily in the correct order. We then run through the sequence of transformations $T_1, \ldots T_j$, applying each obligatory one and perhaps certain optional ones. These transformations may re-arrange strings or may add or delete morphemes. As a result they yield a string of words. We then run through the morphophonemic rules, thereby converting this string of words into a string of phonemes. The phrase structure segment of the grammar will include such rules as those of (4), (8) and (18). The transformational part will include such rules as (16), (19) and (24), formulated properly in the terms that must be developed in a full-scale theory of transformations. The morphophonemic part will include such rules as (9). This sketch of the process of generation of sentences must (and easily can) be generalized to allow for proper functioning of such rules as (16) which operate on a set of sentences, and to allow transformations to reapply to transforms so that more and more complex sentences can be produced.

When we apply only obligatory transformations in the generation of a given sentence, we call the resulting sentence a kernel sentence. Further investigation would show that in the phrase structure and morphophonemic parts of the grammar we can also extract a skeleton of obligatory rules that *must* be applied whenever we reach them in the process of generating a sentence. The phrase structure rules lead to a conception of linguistic structure and 'level of representation' that is fundamentally different from that provided by the morphophonemic rules. On each of the lower levels corresponding to the lower third of the grammar an utterance is, in general, represented by a single sequence of elements. But phrase structure cannot be broken down into sublevels; on the level of phrase structure an utterance is represented by a set of strings that cannot be ordered into higher or lower levels. This set of representing strings is equivalent to a diagram of the form (6). On the transformational level, an utterance is represented even more abstractly in terms of a sequence of transformations by which it is derived, ultimately from kernel sentences (more correctly, from the strings which underlie kernel sentences). There is a very natural general definition of 'linguistic level' that includes all of these cases, and there is good reason to consider each of these structures to be a linguistic level.

When transformational analysis is properly formulated we find that it is essentially more powerful than description in terms of phrase structure, just as the latter is essentially more powerful than description in terms of finite state machines that generate sentences from left to right. In particular, languages which lie beyond the bounds of phrase structure description with context-free rules can be derived transformationally. It is important to observe that the grammar is materially simplified when we add a transformational level, since it is now necessary to provide phrase structure directly only for kernel sentences—the terminal strings of the $[\Sigma, F]$ grammar are just those which underlie kernel sentences. We choose the kernel sentences in such a way that the terminal strings underlying the kernel are easily derived by means of a $[\Sigma, F]$ description, while all other sentences can be derived from these terminal strings by simply statable transformations. We have seen, and shall see again below, several examples of simplifications resulting from transformational analysis. Full-scale syntactic investigation of English provides a great many more cases.

One further point about grammars of the form (25) deserves mention, since it has apparently led to some misunderstanding. We have described these grammars as devices for generating sentences. This formulation has occasionally led to the idea that there is a certain assymmetry in grammatical theory in the sense that grammar is taking the point of view of the speaker rather than the hearer; that it is concerned with the process of producing utterances rather than the 'inverse' process of analysing and reconstructing the structure of given utterances. Actually, grammars of the form that we have been discussing are quite neutral as between speaker and hearer, between synthesis and analysis of utterances. A grammar does not tell us how to synthe-

size a specific utterance; it does not tell us how to analyse a particular
given utterance. In fact, these two tasks which the speaker and hearer
must perform are essentially the same, and are both outside the scope
of grammars of the form (25). Each such grammar is simply a description of a certain set of utterances, namely, those which it generates.
From this grammar we can reconstruct the formal relations that hold
among these utterances in terms of the notions of phrase structure,
transformational structure, etc. Perhaps the issue can be clarified by
an analogy to a part of chemical theory concerned with the structurally
possible compounds. This theory might be said to generate all physically
possible compounds just as a grammar generates all grammatically
'possible' utterances. It would serve as a theoretical basis for techniques
of qualitative analysis and synthesis of specific compounds, just as one
might rely on grammar in the investigation of such special problems
as analysis and synthesis of particular utterances.

After this digression, we can return to the investigation of the
consequences of adopting the transformational approach in the description of English syntax. Our goal is to limit the kernel in such a way
that the terminal strings underlying the kernel sentences are derived
by a simple system of phrase structure and can provide the basis from
which all sentences can be derived by simple transformations: obligatory
transformations in the case of the kernel, obligatory *and* optional
transformations in the case of non-kernel sentences.

To specify a transformation explicitly we must describe the analysis
of the strings to which it applies and the structural change that it
effects on these strings. Thus, the passive transformation applies to
strings of the form *NP–Aux–V–NP* and has the effect of interchanging the two noun phrases, adding *by* before the final noun
phrase, and adding *be+en* to *Aux* (cf. (24)). Consider now the introduction of *not* or *n't* into the auxiliary verb phrase. The simplest way
to describe negation is by means of a transformation which applies
before (19ii) and introduces *not* or *n't* after the second morpheme of
the phrase given by (18iii) if this phrase contains at least two morphemes, or after the first morpheme of this phrase if it contains only
one. Thus this transformation T_{not} operates on strings that are analysed
into three segments in one of the following ways:

(26)   (i)   *NP–C–V* . . .
      (ii) *NP–C+M–* . . .
      (iii) *NP–C+have–* . . .
      (iv) *NP–C+be–* . . .

4

where the symbols are as in (18), (19), and it is immaterial what stands in place of the dots. Given a string analysed into three segments in one of these ways, T_{not} adds *not* (or *n't*) after the second segment of the string. For example, applied to the terminal string *they—Ø+ can—come* (an instance of (26ii)), T_{not} gives *they—Ø+can+n't—come* (ultimately, 'they can't come'); applied to *they—Ø+have+en+come* (an instance of (26iii)), it gives *they—Ø+have+n't—en+come* (ultimately, 'they haven't come'); applied to *they—Ø+be—ing+come* (an instance of (26iv)), it gives *they—Ø+be+n't—ing+come* (ultimately, 'they aren't coming'). The rule thus works properly when we select the last three cases of (26).

Suppose now, that we select an instance of (26i), i.e. a terminal string such as

(27)   *John—S—come*.

which would give the kernel sentence 'John comes' by (19ii). Applied to (27), T_{not} yields

(28)   *John—S+n't—come*.

But we specified that T_{not} applies before (19ii), which has the effect of rewriting $Af+v$ as $v+Af\#$. However, we see that (19ii) does not apply at all to (28) since (28) does not now contain a sequence $Af+v$. Let us now add to the grammar the following obligatory transformational rule which applies *after* (19):

(29) $\#Af \rightarrow \#do+Af$

where *do* is the same element as the main verb in 'John does his homework'. (Cf. (19iii) for introduction of $\#$.) What (29) states is that *do* is introduced as the 'bearer' of an unaffixed affix. Applying (29) and morphological rules to (28) we derive 'John doesn't come'. The rules (26) and (29) now enable us to derive all and only the grammatical forms of sentence negation.

As it stands, the transformational treatment of negation is somewhat simpler than any alternative treatment within phrase structure. The advantage of the transformational treatment (over inclusion of negatives in the kernel) would become much clearer if we could find other cases in which the same formulations (i.e. (26) and (29)) are required for independent reasons. But in fact there are such cases.

Consider the class of 'yes-or-no' questions such as 'have they arrived', 'can they arrive', 'did they arrive'. We can generate all (and only) these sentences by means of a transformation T_q that operates on strings with the analysis (26), and has the effect of interchanging the first and second segments of these strings, as these segments are defined in (26). We require that T_q apply *after* (19i) and *before* (19ii). Applied to

(30)   (i) *they–Ø–arrive*
       (ii) *they–Ø+can–arrive*
      (iii) *they–Ø+have–en+arrive*
     (iv) *they–Ø+be–ing+arrive*

which are of the forms (26i–iv), T_q yields the strings

(31)   (i) *Ø–they–arrive*
      (ii) *Ø+can–they–arrive*
     (iii) *Ø+have–they–en+arrive*
     (iv) *Ø+be–they ing+arrive.*

Applying to these the obligatory rules (19ii, iii) and (29), and then the morphophonemic rules, we derive

(32)   (i) do they arrive
      (ii) can they arrive
     (iii) have they arrived
     (iv) are they arriving

in phonemic transcription. Had we applied the obligatory rules directly to (30), with no intervening T_q, we would have derived the sentences

(33)   (i) they arrive
      (ii) they can arrive
     (iii) they have arrived
     (iv) they are arriving.

Thus (32i–iv) are the interrogative counterparts to (33i–iv).

In the case of (31i), *do* is introduced by rule (29) as the bearer of the unaffixed element *Ø*. If C had been developed into S or *past* by rule (19i), rule (29) would have introduced *do* as a bearer of these elements, and we would have such sentences as 'does he arrive', 'did he arrive'. Note that no new morphophonemic rules are needed to account for the fact that $do + Ø→/duw/$, $do +S→/dəz/$, $do +past→/did/$; we need these rules anyway to account for the forms of *do* as a main verb. Notice also that T_q must apply after (19i), or number will not be assigned correctly in questions.

In analysing the auxiliary verb phrase in rules (18), (19), we considered S to be the morpheme of the third person singular and *Ø* to be the morpheme affixed to the verb for all other forms of the subject. Thus the verb has S if the noun subject has $\emptyset$ ('the boy arrives') and the verb has $\emptyset$ if the subject has S ('the boys arrive'). An alternative that we did not consider was to eleminate the zero morpheme and to state simply that *no* affix occurs if the subject is not third person singular. We see now that this alternative is not acceptable. We must have the $\emptyset$ morpheme or there will be no affix in (30i) for *do* to bear, and rule (29) will thus not apply to (31i). There are many other cases where transformational analysis provides compelling reasons for or against the establishment of zero morphemes. As a negative case, consider the suggestion that intransitive verbs be analysed as verbs with zero object. But then the passive transformation (24) would convert, e.g. 'John–slept– $\emptyset$' into the non-sentence '$\emptyset$–was slept–by John'→'was slept by John'. Hence this analysis of intransitives must be rejected.

The crucial fact about the question transformation T_q is that almost nothing must be added to the grammar in order to describe it. Since both the subdivision of the sentence that it imposes and the rule for appearance of *do* were required independently for negation, we need only describe the inversion effected by T_q in extending the grammar to account for yes-or-no questions. Putting it differently, transformational analysis brings out the fact that negatives and interrogatives have fundamentally the same 'structure', and it can make use of this fact to simplify the description of English syntax.

Syntactic Structures, 35–48, 61–5

3 Syntax: II

3.1 *Introductory*

[In the previous section we described a version of transformational grammar which became widely known as a result of the publication of *Syntactic Structures* in 1957. During the following years the application of transformational theory to the description of natural languages was actively pursued, and as a result of this work it became clear that the original formulation of the grammar required a number of modifications. These modifications were incorporated into *Aspects of the Theory of Syntax* (1965). Important changes in the theory were apparent in the representation of lexical categories and the relationship between the lexicon and the rest of the grammar, the introduction of separate phonological and semantic components, and in the reformulation of the transformational component of the grammar. As a result of these modifications the concept of kernel sentences, and of a set of optional transformations applying to the underlying forms of kernel sentences to produce more complex sentences, was abandoned. The extracts in this section deal with the revised version of transformational grammar as it appeared in *Aspects* in 1965. [A, B]]

3.2 *Categories and relations*

The investigation of generative grammar can profitably begin with a careful analysis of the kind of information presented in traditional grammars. Adopting this as a heuristic procedure, let us consider what a traditional grammar has to say about a simple English sentence such as the following:

(1)   sincerity may frighten the boy

Concerning this sentence, a traditional grammar might provide information of the following sort:

(2) (i)   the string (1) is a Sentence (S); *frighten the boy* is a Verb
Phrase (VP) consisting of the Verb (V) *frighten* and the

Noun Phrase (NP) *the boy; sincerity* is also an NP; the NP *the boy* consists of the Determiner (Det) *the,* followed by a Noun (N); the NP *sincerity* consists of just an N; *the* is, furthermore, an Article (Art); *may* is a Verbal Auxiliary (Aux) and, furthermore, a Modal (M).

(ii) the NP *sincerity* functions as the Subject of the sentence (1), whereas the VP *frighten the boy* functions as the Predicate of this sentence; the NP *the boy* functions as the Object of the VP, and the V *frighten* as its Main Verb; the grammatical relation Subject-Verb holds of the pair (*sincerity, frighten*), and the grammatical relation Verb-Object holds of the pair (*frighten, the boy*).

(iii) the N *boy* is a Count Noun (as distinct from the Mass Noun *butter* and the Abstract Noun *sincerity*) and a Common Noun (as distinct from the Proper Noun *John* and the Pronoun *it*); it is, furthermore, an Animate Noun (as distinct from *book*) and a Human Noun (as distinct from *bee*); *frighten* is a Transitive Verb (as distinct from *occur*), and one that does not freely permit Object deletion (as distinct from *read, eat*); it takes Progressive Aspect freely (as distinct from *know, own*); it allows Abstract Subjects (as distinct from *eat, admire*) and Human Objects (as distinct from *read, wear*).

It seems to me that the information presented in (2) is, without question, substantially correct and is essential to any account of how the language is used or acquired. The main topic I should like to consider is how information of this sort can be formally presented in a structural description, and how such structural descriptions can be generated by a system of explicit rules.

The remarks given in (2i) concern the subdivision of the string (1) into continuous substrings, each of which is assigned to a certain category. Information of this sort can be represented by a labelled bracketing of (1), or, equivalently, by a tree-diagram such as (3).

(3)

If one assumes now that (1) is a basic string, the structure represented as (3) can be taken as a first approximation to its (base) Phrase-marker.

A grammar that generates simple Phrase-markers such as (3) may be based on a vocabulary of symbols that includes both *formatives* (*the*, *boy*, etc.) and *category symbols* (S, NP, V, etc.). The formatives, furthermore, can be subdivided into *lexical* items (*sincerity*, *boy*) and *grammatical* items (*Perfect*, *Possessive*, etc.; except possibly for *the*, none of these are represented in the simplified example given).

To provide a Phrase-marker such as (3), the base component might contain the following sequence of rewriting rules:

(4) (I) S→NP⌢Aux⌢VP*   (II) M→*may*
         VP→V⌢NP   N→*sincerity*
         NP→Det⌢N   N→*boy*
         NP→N   V→*frighten*
         Det→*the*
         Aux→M

Notice that the rules (4), although they do suffice to generate (3), will also generate such deviant strings as *boy may frighten the sincerity*. This is a problem to which we shall turn below.

There is a natural distinction in (4) between rules that introduce lexical formatives (class (II)) and the others. In fact, we shall see that it is necessary to distinguish these sets and to assign the lexical rules to a distinct subpart of the base of the syntactic component.

In the case of the information in (2i), then, we see quite clearly how it is to be formally represented, and what sorts of rules are required to generate these representations.

[Turning now to (2ii), we see that the notions in question have an entirely different status. The notion 'Subject', as distinct from the notion 'NP', designates a *grammatical function* rather than a *grammatical category*. A grammatical function is an inherently relational notion. In traditional terms we say that in (1) *sincerity* belongs to the category NP and that it functions as the Subject of the sentence. Chomsky proposes that we define the notion 'Subject of' as [NP, S] and say, with respect to Phrase-marker (3), that *sincerity* is the Subject of the sentence *sincerity may frighten the boy* by virtue of the fact that it is NP

---

* The symbol ⌢ has the same function as +. [A, B]

which is directly dominated by S in the Phrase-marker associated with the sentence. Similarly, the following definitions are proposed:

(5)   (i) 'Predicate of': [VP, S]
     (ii) 'Direct Object of': [NP, VP]
     (iii) 'Main Verb of': [V, VP]

We can now say that *frighten the boy* is the Predicate of the sentence, and that *the boy* is the Direct Object of the Verb Phrase *frighten the boy* and *frighten* is its Main Verb. Grammatical relations of the sort that hold between *sincerity* and *frighten* (Subject-Verb) and between *frighten* and *boy* (Verb-Object) in (1) are defined derivatively in terms of the functional notions already established. Thus Subject-Verb is defined as the relation between the Subject of a Sentence and the Main Verb of the Predicate of the Sentence, and Verb-Object is defined as the relation between the Main Verb of and the Direct Object of a VP. In this way Chomsky attempts to extract information concerning grammatical function of the sort exemplified in (2ii) directly from the rewriting rules of the base, so as to avoid having to elaborate the rules in order to provide specific mention of grammatical function*.]

3.3 *Syntactic features and context-sensitive rules*

Consider now how information of the sort given in (2iii) can be presented in explicit rules. Note that this information concerns *sub-*

---

* In practice the sharp distinction between function and category is difficult to maintain. For example, a fragment of the base component of a grammar of English given in *Aspects* contains the rule:

$$\text{Predicate-Phrase} \rightarrow \text{Aux} + \text{VP (Place) (Time)}.$$

If function labels are not allowed in the base component, presumably the labels 'Place' and 'Time' should not appear here. On the other hand, if we replace both labels by the syntactic category Prep-Phrase, which strictly speaking is required by the theory, it is not clear how we would show that basically 'place comes before time' in English (e.g. 'He was working in London at the time his father died'). Furthermore, for various technical reasons rules of the type:

$$\left\{ \begin{array}{c} \text{Time} \\ \text{Place} \end{array} \right\} \rightarrow \text{Prep-Phrase}$$

are undesirable in the base component of transformational grammars. How then are we to state that adverbial phrases of time and place are deep prepositional phrases? In other words, if we try to maintain Chomsky's strict distinction between function and category, we seem either to lose categorial information or to generate ungrammatical sentences. It is difficult to avoid the conclusion that thi problem constitutes a gap in the theory at the present time. How serious and cruscial a gap this might be remains to be seen. [A, B] *categorization* rather than 'branching' (that is, analysis of a category into a sequence of categories, as when S is analysed into NP⌢Aux⌢ VP, or NP into Det⌢N). Furthermore, it seems that the only categories involved are those containing lexical formatives as members. Hence, we are dealing with a rather restricted part of grammatical structure, and it is important to bear this in mind in exploring appropriate means for presenting these facts.

The obvious suggestion is to deal with subcategorization by rewriting rules of the type described on page 45, and this was the assumption made in the first attempts to formalize generative grammars. However, G. H. Matthews, in the course of his work on a generative grammar of German in 1957–8, pointed out that this assumption was incorrect and that rewriting rules are not the appropriate device to effect subcategorization of lexical categories. The difficulty is that this subcategorization is typically not strictly hierarchic, but involves rather cross classification. Thus, for example, Nouns in English are either Proper (*John, Egypt*) or Common (*boy, book*) and either Human (*John, boy*) or non-Human (*Egypt, book*). Certain rules (for example, some involving Determiners) apply to the Proper/Common distinction; others (for example, rules involving choice of Relative Pronoun) to the Human/non-Human distinction. But if the subcategorization is given by rewriting rules, then one or the other of these distinctions will have to dominate, and the other will be unstatable in the natural way. Thus if we decide to take Proper/Common as the major distinction, we have such rules as

(6)   N→Proper
       N→Common
       Proper→Pr-Human
       Proper→Pr-nHuman
       Common→C-Human
       Common→C-nHuman

where the symbols 'Pr-Human', 'Pr-nHuman', 'C-Human', and 'C-nHuman' are entirely unrelated, as distinct from one another as the symbols 'Noun', 'Verb', 'Adjective', and 'Modal'. In this system, although we can easily state a rule that applies only to Proper Nouns or only to Common Nouns, a rule that applies to Human Nouns must be stated in terms of the unrelated categories Pr-Human and C-Human. This obviously indicates that a generalization is being missed, since this rule would now be no simpler or better motivated than, for example, a rule applying to the unrelated categories Pr-Human and Abstract Nouns. As the depth of the analysis increases, problems of this sort mount to the point where they indicate a serious inadequacy in a grammar that consists only of rewriting rules. Nor is this particular difficulty overcome, as many others are, when we add transformational rules to the grammar.

Formally, this problem is identical to one that is familiar on the level of phonology. Thus phonological units are also cross-classified, with respect to phonological rules. There are, for example, rules that apply to voiced consonants [b], [z], but not to unvoiced consonants [p], [s], and there are other rules that apply to continuants [s], [z], but not to stops [p], [b], and so on. For this reason it is necessary to regard each phonological unit as a set of features, and to design the phonological component in such a way that each rule applies to all segments containing a certain feature or constellation of features. (See section 4 for a more detailed discussion of phonological rules.)

These notions can be adapted without essential change to the representation of lexical categories and their members, providing a very natural solution to the cross-classification problem and, at the same time, contributing to the general unity of grammatical theory. Each lexical formative will have associated with it a set of *syntactic features* (thus *boy* will have the syntactic features [+Common], [+ Human], etc.). Furthermore, the symbols representing lexical categories (N, V, etc.) will be analysed by the rules into *complex symbols*, each complex symbol being a set of specified syntactic features, just as each phonological segment is a set of specified phonological features. For example, we might have the following grammatical rules:

(7) (i)   N→[+N, ± Common]
     (ii) [+Common]→[± Count]
     (iii) [+Count]→[± Animate]
     (iv) [−Common]→[± Animate]
     (v)   [+Animate]→[± Human]
     (vi) [−Count]→[± Abstract]

We interpret rule (7) as asserting that the symbol N in a line of a derivation is to be replaced by one of the two *complex symbols* [+N, +Common] or [+N, −Common]. The rules (7ii–7vi) operate under the conventions for phonological rules. Thus rule (7ii) asserts that any complex symbol Q that is already specified as [+Common] is to be replaced by the complex symbol containing all of the features of Q along with either the feature specification [+Count] or [−Count]. The same is true of the other rules that operate on complex symbols.

The total effect of the rules (7) can be represented by the branching diagram (8). In this representation, each node is labelled by a feature,

(8)

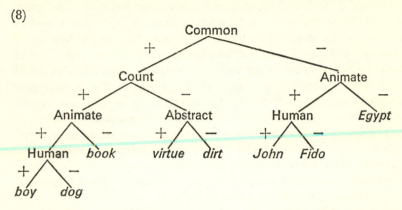

and the lines are labelled + or −. Each maximal path corresponds to a category of lexical items; an element of this category has the feature [aF] (a = + or −) if and only if one of the lines constituting this path is labelled a and descends from a node labelled F. Typical members of the categories defined by (7) are given at the terminal points of (8).

A system of complex symbol rules need not be representable by a branching diagram of this sort. For example, the categories defined by the rules (7) are also defined by the rules (9), but in this case there is no representing branching diagram.

(9) (i) N→[+N, ±Animate, ±Common]
     (ii) [+Common]→[±Count]
     (iii) [−Count]→$\begin{bmatrix} \pm \text{Abstract} \\ -\text{Animate} \end{bmatrix}$
     (iv) [+Animate]→[±Human]

If we were to require representability in a branching diagram as a formal condition of these rules, then (9) would be excluded. In this case, the rules could just as well be presented in the form (8) as the form (9). In any event, with rules of this sort that introduce and elaborate complex symbols, we can develop the full set of lexical categories.

We now modify the description of the base subcomponent that was presented earlier, and exemplified by (4), in the following way. In addition to rewriting rules that apply to category symbols and that generally involve branching, there are rewriting rules such as (7) that apply to symbols for lexical categories and that introduce or operate on complex symbols (sets of specified syntactic features). The grammar will now contain no rules such as those of (4II) that introduce the formatives belonging to lexical categories. Instead the base of the grammar will contain a *lexicon*, which is simply an unordered list of all lexical formatives. More precisely, the lexicon is a set of *lexical entries*, each lexical entry being a pair (D, C); where D is a phonological distinctive feature matrix 'spelling' a certain lexical formative, and C is a collection of specified syntactic features (a complex symbol).

The system of rewriting rules will now generate derivations terminating with strings that consist of grammatical formatives and complex symbols. Such a string we call a *preterminal string*. A terminal string is formed from a preterminal string by insertion of a lexical formative in accordance with the following *lexical rule*:

If Q is a complex symbol of a preterminal string and (D, C) is a lexical entry, where C is not distinct from Q, then Q can be replaced by D.

As a concrete example, consider again the sentence *sincerity may frighten the boy* ($= (1)$). Instead of the grammar (4) we now have a grammar containing the branching rules (4I), which I repeat here as (10), along with the subcategorization rules (7), repeated as (11), and containing a lexicon with the entries (12). It is to be understood, here and later on, that the italicized items stand for phonological distinctive feature matrices, that is, 'spellings' of formatives.

(10)   S→NP⌢Aux⌢VP
       VP→V⌢P
       NP→Det⌢N
       NP→N
       Det→*the*
       Aux→M

(11)   (i) N→[+N, ± Common]
      (ii) [+Common]→[± Count]
     (iii) [+Count]→[± Animate]
      (iv) [−Common]→[± Animate]
       (v) [+Animate]→[± Human]
      (vi) [−Count]→[± Abstract]

(12)   (*sincerity*, [+N, −Count, +Abstract])
       (*boy*, [+N, +Count, +Common, +Animate, +Human])
       (*may*, [+M])

These rules allow us to generate the preterminal string

(13)   [+N, −Count, +Abstract] ⌢ M ⌢ Q ⌢ *the* ⌢ [+N, +Count,
       +Animate, +Human],

where Q is the complex symbol into which V is analysed by rules
that we shall discuss directly. The lexical rule (which, since it is
perfectly general, need not be stated in any grammar—in other words,
it constitutes part of the definition of 'derivation') now allows us to
insert *sincerity* for the first complex symbol and *boy* for the last complex
symbol of (13) and, as we shall see, to insert *frighten* for Q (and *may*
for M). Except for the case of *frighten*, the information about the
sentence (1) that is given in (2) is now explicitly provided in full
by the Phrase-marker generated by the grammar consisting of the
rules (10), (11), and the lexicon (12). We might represent this Phrase-
marker in the form shown in (14). If the lexicon includes additional

(14)

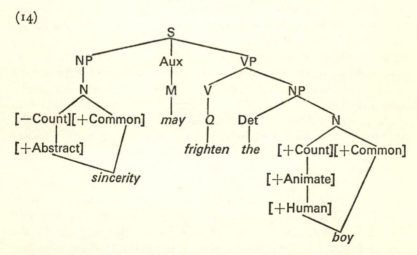

specific information about the lexical items that appear in (13), this
information will also appear in the Phrase-marker, represented in
terms of features that appear in the Phrase-marker in a position
dominated by the lexical categories N and V and dominating the
formative in question.

We can see immediately that separating the lexicon from the

system of rewriting rules has quite a number of advantages. For one thing, many of the grammatical properties of formatives can now be specified directly in the lexicon, by association of syntactic features with lexical formatives, and thus need not be represented in the rewriting rules at all. In particular, morphological properties of various kinds can be treated in this way—for example, membership of lexical items in derivational classes (declensional classes, strong or weak verbs, nominalizable adjectives, etc.). Since many such properties are entirely irrelevant to the functioning of the rules of the base and are, furthermore, highly idiosyncratic, the grammar can be significantly simplified if they are excluded from the rewriting rules and listed in lexical entries, where they most naturally belong. Or, returning to (2iii), notice that it is now unnecessary to use rewriting rules to classify Transitive Verbs into those that do and those that do not normally permit Object deletion. Instead, the lexical entries for *read, eat,* on the one hand, and *frighten, keep,* on the other, will differ in specification for the particular syntactic feature of Object deletion, which is not mentioned in the rewriting rules at all. The transformational rule that deletes Objects will now be applicable only to those words positively specified with respect to this feature, this information now being contained in the Phrase-marker of the strings in which these words appear. Any attempt to construct a careful grammar will quickly reveal that many formatives have unique or almost unique grammatical characteristics, so that the simplification of the grammar that can be effected in these ways will certainly be substantial.

In general, all properties of a formative that are essentially idiosyncratic will be specified in the lexicon. In particular, the lexical entry must specify: (*a*) aspects of phonetic structure that are not predictable by general rule (for example, in the case of *bee*, the phonological matrix of the lexical entry will specify that the first segment is a voiced labial stop and the second an acute vowel, but it will not specify the degree of aspiration of the stop or the fact that the vowel is voiced, tense, and unrounded); (*b*) properties relevant to the functioning of transformational rules (as the example of the preceding paragraph, and many others); (*c*) properties of the formative that are relevant for semantic interpretation (that is, components of the dictionary definition); (*d*) lexical features indicating the positions in which a lexical formative can be inserted (by the lexical rule) in a preterminal string. In short, it contains information that is required by the phonological and semantic components of the grammar and by the transformational part of the syntactic component of the grammar, as well as information that determines the proper placement of lexical entries in sentences, and hence, by implication, the degree and manner of deviation of strings that are not directly generated.

It is important to observe that the base system no longer is, strictly speaking, a phrase structure (constituent structure) grammar. As described in section 2.2, a phrase structure grammar consists of an unordered set of rewriting rules, and assigns a structural description that can be represented as a tree-diagram with nodes labelled by symbols of the vocabulary. This theory formalizes a conception of linguistic structure that is substantive and interesting, and that has been quite influential for at least half a century, namely the 'taxonomic' view that syntactic structure is determined exclusively by operations of segmentations and classification. Of course, we have already departed from this theory by assuming that the rewriting rules apply in a prescribed sequence to generate a restricted set of (base) strings, rather than freely to generate the full set of actual sentences. This modification restricted the role of the phrase structure grammar. But introduction of complex symbols constitutes another radical departure from this theory, and the separate treatment of the lexicon just suggested is again an essential revision.

We have not yet considered how the category V is analysed into a complex symbol. Thus suppose that we have the grammar (10)–(12). We must still give rules to determine whether a V may or may not be transitive, and so on, and must add to the lexicon appropriate entries for individual verbal formatives. It would not do simply to add to the grammar the rule (15), analogous to (11):

(15)   V→[+V, ± Progressive, ± Transitive, ± Abstract-Subject,
         ± Animate-Object]

The problem is that an occurrence of the category symbol V can be replaced by a complex symbol containing the feature [+Transitive] just in case it is in the environment ——NP. Similarly, the Verb can be positively specified for the feature [Abstract-Subject] just in case it is in the environment [+Abstract] . . .——; and it can be positively specified for the feature [Animate-Object] just in case it is in the environment ——. . . [+Animate]; and so on, in the case of all those lexical features that are involved in the statement of contextual restrictions. Hence, the features [Transitive], [Abstract-Subject], [Animate-Object] must be introduced by rewriting rules that are restricted with respect to context, as distinct from the context-free rules (9) that subcategorize Nouns.

Observe that the feature specification [+Transitive] can be regarded as merely a notation indicating occurrence in the environment ——NP. A more expressive notation would be simply the symbol '——NP' itself. Generalizing, let us allow certain features to be designated in the form [X——Y], where X and Y are strings (perhaps null) of symbols. We shall henceforth call these *contextual features*. Let us regard Transitive Verbs as positively specified for the contextual feature [——NP], pre-Adjectival Verbs such as *grow, feel*, as positively specified for the contextual feature [——Adjective], and so on. We then have a general rule of subcategorization to the effect that *a Verb is positively specified with respect to the contextual feature associated with the context in which it occurs.*

[Thus, in the case of Verb subclassification, we shall have the rule (16), which expresses the fact that the set of frames in which the symbol V occurs imposes a corresponding subclassification on V, with one subdivision corresponding to each listed context ('CS' stands for 'complex symbol')]:

(16)

$$V \rightarrow CS/\text{——}\left\{\begin{array}{l} \text{NP} \\ \# \\ \text{Adjective} \\ \text{Predicate-Nominal} \\ like\frown\text{Predicate-Nominal} \\ \text{Prepositional-Phrase} \\ that\frown\text{S}'\text{*} \\ \text{NP (of}\frown\text{Det}\frown\text{N) S}' \\ \text{etc.} \end{array}\right\}$$

The lexicon might now contain the items

(17)   *eat*, [+V, +——NP]
       elapse, [+V, +—— #]
       grow, [+V, +——NP, +—— #, +——Adjective]
       become, [+V, +——Adjective, +——Predicate-Nominal]
       seem, [+V, +——Adjective, +——*like*$\frown$Predicate-Nominal]

---

* The status of the symbol S′ in this rule is unexplained at the present state of the exposition. It will indicate the position of a transform of a sentence, as the theory of syntactic component is extended later on. [C]

look, [+V, +——(Prepositional-Phrase) #, +——Adjective,
      +——*like*⌢Predicate-Nominal]
believe, [+V, +——NP, +——*that*⌢S']
persuade, [+V, +——NP (*of*⌢Det⌢N) S']

and so on. The rules (16) supplemented by the lexicon (17) will permit such expressions as *John eats food, a week elapsed, John grew a beard, John grew, John grew sad, John became sad, John became president, John seems sad, John seems like a nice fellow, John looked, John looked at Bill, John looks sad, John looks like a nice fellow, John believes me, John believes that it is unlikely, John persuaded Bill that we should leave, John persuaded Bill of the necessity for us to leave.*

We see that with a slight extension of conventional notations the systematic use of complex symbols permits a fairly simple and informative statement of one of the basic processes of subclassification.

We can use the same notational device to assign features of the Subject and Object to the Verb.

$$
(18) \quad
\left.
\begin{array}{l}
\text{(i)} \\
\text{(ii)} \\
\text{(iii)} \\
\text{(iv)}
\end{array}
\right\}
[+V] \to CS /
\left\{
\begin{array}{l}
[+\text{Abstract}]\ \text{Aux}\text{——} \\
[-\text{Abstract}]\ \text{Aux}\text{——} \\
\text{——Det}\ [+\text{Animate}] \\
\text{——Det}\ [-\text{Animate}]
\end{array}
\right\}
$$

The rules of (16) and (18) analyse a category into a complex symbol in terms of the frame in which this category appears. The rules differ in that in the case of (16) the frame is stated in terms of category symbols, whereas in the case of (18) the frame is stated in terms of syntactic features. Rules such as (16), which analyse a symbol in terms of its categorial context, I shall henceforth call *strict subcategorization rules*. Rules such as (18), which analyse a symbol (generally, a complex symbol) in terms of syntactic features of the frames in which it appears, I shall call *selectional rules*. The latter express what are usually called 'selectional restrictions' or 'restrictions of co-occurrence'.

Aspects of the Theory of Syntax, 63–5, 67–8, 79–80, 82–8, 90, 93–5

3.4 *Deep structures and grammatical transformations*

[In *Syntactic Structures* Chomsky uses a set of context-restricted phrase structure rules to generate the underlying structures of kernel sentences. Transformations of various kinds then operate on the underlying structures of kernel sentences to produce more complex sentences.

In order to ensure that the phrase structure rules assign a perfectly clear and unambiguous constituent structure to every string of elements that they generate, it is necessary to place certain constraints on the rules. Thus, the phrase structure rules can replace a single symbol by a sequence of one or more other symbols, but the rules cannot delete elements, rearrange the order of elements, or expand more than one symbol at a time. These restrictions ensure that we can trace the exact derivational history of every string generated by the phrase structure rules, and this in turn enables us to formulate transformational rules stating that we may bring about changes in the terminal string of a phrase structure grammar if, and only if, the string has a certain derivational history recorded in the Phrase-marker associated with it.

A Phrase-marker exactly specifies the structural relationships between all the elements at any level in the structure of a sentence by means of the correlative concepts 'dominates' and 'is a'. Thus, with reference to (6) on p. 25, we can say that 'the ball' is an NP, or that Verb+NP is a VP, or that NP+VP is a Sentence, etc. The relationship 'dominates' is the inverse of 'is a'. Thus Sentence dominates NP+VP, VP dominates Verb+NP, NP dominates T+N, etc. The conditions on phrase structure rules ensure that these relationships can be determined directly from the derivation.

Transformations can be *singular* (operating on a single Phrase-marker) or *generalized* (operating on two or more Phrase-markers to produce a single new Phrase-marker by a process of embedding or conjoining). The following pairs of sentences represent singular transformations:

(19)   (i) John kissed Mary→Mary was kissed by John.

   (ii) They will win→Will they win?

   (iii) The problem was difficult→The problem wasn't difficult.

The following sentences represent generalized transformations:

(20)   (i) The man stayed for supper⎫ →The man who bought the
       The man bought the house⎭   house stayed for supper.

   (ii) He said it   ⎫
        He was going   ⎬ →He said that he was going.
                       ⎭

   (iii) We have to work hard ⎫ →Our having to work hard is a
         It is a nuisance   ⎭   nuisance.

In the above examples we have used actual sentences in place of the abstract structures that underlie sentences, and are converted into sentences by transformational processes. This convention is often adopted in informal presentations. It should be borne in mind, however, that strictly speaking transformations are defined not on sentences or their surface structures, but on Phrase-markers that are more abstract.

The passive transformation of *Syntactic Structures* is usually given in the form:

(21) $NP_1 + Aux + V + NP_2 \rightarrow NP_2 + Aux + be + en + V + by + NP_1$

The string to the left of the arrow is called the *structural description* and the operation indicated by the rule is called the *structural change*. Whereas phrase structure rules apply only to the output of the rule previously applied, transformational rules apply to all strings that are *analysable* in terms of the elements referred to in the structural description. Thus in the case of the passive transformation, if a string is analysable without remainder into four substrings, and these substrings are dominated in the Phrase-marker associated with the string by the symbols NP, Aux, V and NP respectively, then the string satisfies the conditions defined by the structural description, and falls within the domain of the passive transformation. It is a characteristic of many transformational rules that at least one of the symbols in the structural description functions as a variable which may take as its value any one of the substrings dominated by that symbol in the Phrase-marker associated with the string. Thus, in the case of the passive transformation, NP functions as a variable which may take as its value any of the substrings generated by the phrase structure rules and dominated by NP, including the substrings which are ultimately realized as *the girl, the girl next door, that pretty girl who came to the party in a sports car,* and countless others.

In the following extract Chomsky argues that the operation of the rules in the semantic component will be simplified if all the information necessary for semantic interpretation is present in a base Phrase-marker. In this case, to account for example for declarative and interrogative sentences, the rewriting rules in the base component must generate both the Phrase-markers (22) and (23), where (23) is the Phrase-marker underlying the sentence *Did John kiss Mary?* and the constituent Q indicates that the surface structure is interpreted semantically as a question:

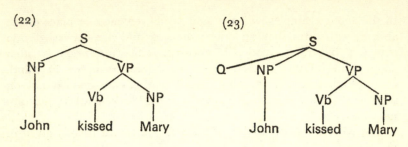

(22)   (23)

If the rewriting rules in the base are made to operate in this way, the optional singulary question transformation of *Syntactic Structures* becomes an obligatory transformation which applies whenever the marker 'Q' appears in a phrase structure terminal string. The principle extends to imperative and negative transformations which also become obligatory rules applying whenever the appropriate marker, Imp or Neg, appears in a phrase structure terminal string. The effect of these changes is to eliminate most optional transformational rules from the grammar and to ensure that transformations play no part in semantic interpretation. Semantic interpretation now depends solely on the lexical items in a sentence and the grammatical functions and relations represented in the underlying structures*.

In the revised version of the grammar the rewriting, or categorial, rules in the base component are context-free. These rules generate an infinite set of *generalized Phrase-markers*, i.e. clusters of single Phrase-markers together with a specification of the way in which the Phrase-markers are embedded and conjoined. Since the categorial rules are context-free, with no distributional restrictions on the embedding of one Phrase-marker into another, it is evident that the base rules will generate many generalized Phrase-markers which do not underlie any acceptable surface structure. Consequently it becomes a function of the transformational rules, operating in a cycle, to 'filter out' all generalized Phrase-markers which are not well-formed, and which do not qualify as the deep structures of sentences.

Suppose, then, that the base of the grammar is divided into two parts, a *categorial component* and a *lexicon*. The primary role of the categorial component is to define implicitly the basic grammatical relations that function in the deep structure of the language.]

The base will now generate base Phrase-markers. The basis of a

---

* This part of the standard theory has now been modified. See section 5.1. [A, B]

sentence is the sequence of base Phrase-markers that underlies it. The basis of a sentence is mapped into the sentence by the transformational rules, which, furthermore, automatically assign to the sentence a derived Phrase-marker (ultimately, a surface structure) in the process.

For concreteness, consider a base component which generates the Phrase-markers (24)–(25)*. The base Phrase-marker (26), with a different choice of Auxiliary, would be the basis for the sentence 'John was examined by a specialist'. The Phrase-marker (24) would be the basis for the sentence 'the man was fired', were we to modify it by deleting S' from the Determiner associated with *man*. (In this case, the passive transformation is followed by the deletion of unspecified agent.) As it stands, however, to form the basis of some sentence, the base Phrase-marker (24) must be supplemented by another Phrase-marker, a transform of which will fill the position of S' in (24) and thus serve as a relative clause qualifying *man*. Similarly, (25) alone cannot serve as a basis for a sentence because the S' appearing in the Verbal Complement must be replaced by the transform of

(24)

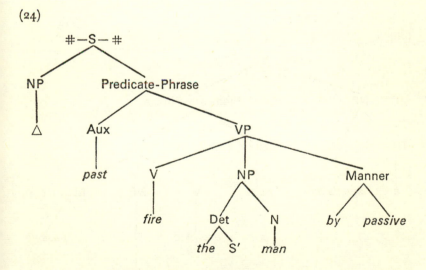

* Some details irrelevant to the problem under discussion are omitted in these examples. We here regard each lexical item as standing for a complex of features. The dummy symbol △ stands for various unspecified elements that will be deleted by obligatory transformations. [C]

(25)

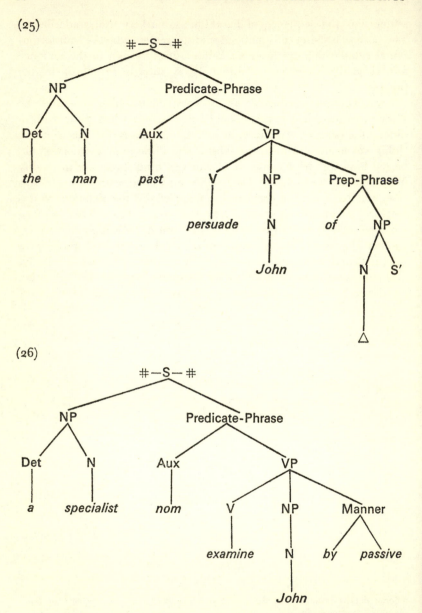

(26)

some other Phrase-marker. In fact, however, the sequence of base Phrase-markers (24), (25), (26) is the basis for the well-formed sentence:

(27)   the man who persuaded John to be examined by a specialist
        was fired.

The 'transformational history' of (27) by which it is derived from
its basis might be represented, informally, by the diagram (28).

(28)

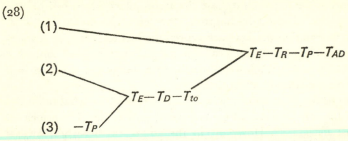

$$(1)\text{---------------------}$$
$$\nearrow T_E - T_R - T_P - T_{AD}$$
$$(2)$$
$$\nearrow T_E - T_D - T_{to}$$
$$(3) \quad -T_P$$

We interpret this as follows: First, apply the Passive transformation
T_P to the base Phrase-marker (26); embed the result in the base
Phrase-marker (25), in place of S′, by a generalized (double-base)
substitution transformation T_E, giving a Phrase-marker for 'the man
persuaded John of △ John *nom* be examined by a specialist'; to this
apply first T_D, which deletes the repeated NP 'John', and then T_{to},
which replaces 'of △ *nom*' by 'to', giving a Phrase-marker for 'the man
persuaded John to be examined by a specialist'; next embed this in
the position of S′ in (24), by T_E; to this apply the relative transformation T_R, which permutes the embedded sentence with the following N
and replaces the repeated phrase 'the man' by 'who', giving a Phrase-
marker for '△ fired the man who persuaded John to be examined by
a specialist by *passive*'; to this Phrase-marker apply the passive transformation and agent deletion (T_{AD}), giving (27).

I have left out of this description quite a few transformations that
are necessary to give the correct form of (27), as well as other details,
but these are, by and large, well known, and introduction of them
changes nothing relevant to this discussion.

The diagram (28) is an informal representation of what we may
call a *Transformation-marker*. It represents the transformational structure
of the utterance (28) very much in the way a Phrase-marker represents
the phrase structure of a terminal string. In fact, a Transformation-
marker may be formally represented as a set of strings in an alphabet
consisting of base Phrase-markers and transformations as its elements,
just as a Phrase-marker may be formally represented as a set of strings
in an alphabet consisting of terminal symbols, category symbols, and
with the developments of the preceding sections, specified features.

The deep structure of an utterance is given completely by its Transformation-marker, which contains its basis. The surface structure of the sentence is the derived Phrase-marker given as the output of the operations represented in the Transformation-marker. The basis of the sentence is the sequence of base Phrase-markers that constitute the terminal points of the tree-diagram (the left-hand nodes, in (28)). When transformation-markers are represented as in (28), the branching points correspond to generalized transformations that embed a constituent sentence (the lower branch) in a designated position in a matrix sentence (the upper branch).

A theoretical apparatus of this sort, in its essentials, is what underlies the work in transformational generative grammar that has appeared in the last ten years*. However, in the course of this work, several important points have gradually emerged which suggest that a somewhat more restricted and conceptually simpler theory of transformations may be adequate.

First, it has been shown that many of the optional singulary transformations of *Syntactic Structures* must be reformulated as obligatory transformations, whose applicability to a string is determined by presence or absence of a certain marker in the string. This was pointed out by Lees (1960) for the negation transformation, and by Klima (personal communication) for the question transformation, at about the same time. In fact, it is also true for the passive transformation. Katz and Postal (1964) have extended these observations and formulated them in terms of a general principle, namely that *the only contribution of transformations to semantic interpretation is that they interrelate Phrase-markers* (i.e. combine semantic interpretations of already interpreted Phrase-markers in a fixed way). It follows, then, that transformations cannot introduce meaning-bearing elements (nor can they delete lexical items unrecoverably). Generalizing these remarks to embedding transformations, they conclude also that a sentence transform embedded in a matrix sentence Σ must replace a dummy symbol of Σ. (In the foregoing discussion, adopting this suggestion, we have used S′ as the dummy symbol—this assumption is also implicit in Fillmore, 1963.)

Katz and Postal point out that the principle just stated greatly simplifies the theory of the semantic component, since semantic interpretation will now be independent of all aspects of the

---

* Published in 1965.

Transformation-marker except insofar as this indicates how base structures are interrelated. They have also succeeded in showing that in a large variety of cases, where this general principle has not been met in syntactic description, the description was in fact incorrect on internal syntactic grounds. The principle, then, seems very plausible.

Second, notice that the theory of Transformation-markers permits a great deal of latitude so far as ordering of transformations is concerned. Thus the grammar, in this view, must contain rules generating the possible Transformation-markers by stating conditions that these objects must meet for well-formedness (what Lees, 1960, calls 'traffic rules'). These rules may state the ordering of transformations relative to one another, and may designate certain transformations as obligatory, or obligatory relative to certain contexts, by requiring that they appear in specified positions in Transformation-markers. However, only some of the possibilities permitted by this general theory have been realized convincingly with actual linguistic material. In particular, there are no known cases of ordering among generalized embedding transformations although such ordering is permitted by the theory of Transformation-markers. Furthermore, there are no really convincing cases of singulary transformations that must apply to a matrix sentence before a sentence transform is embedded in it, though this too is a possibility, according to the theory. On the other hand, there are many examples of ordering of singulary transformations, and many examples of singulary transformations that must apply to a constituent sentence before it is embedded or that must apply to a matrix sentence after embedding of a constituent structure in it. Thus the diagram (28) is typical of the kind of structure that has actually been discovered in Transformation-markers.

In brief, presently available descriptive studies suggest the following restrictions on ordering of transformations. The singulary transformations are linearly ordered (perhaps only partially ordered). They may apply to a constituent structure before it is embedded, or to a matrix structure, and the constituent structure embedded in it, after this constituent structure is embedded. There is no reason for imposing an extrinsic order on the generalized transformations.

These observations suggest a possible simplification of the theory of transformational grammar. Suppose that we eliminate the notions 'generalized transformation' and 'Transformation-marker' altogether. In the rewriting rules of the base (in fact, in its categorial component) the string #S# is introduced in the positions where in the illustrative example we introduced the symbol S'. That is, wherever a base Phrase-marker contains a position in which a sentence transform is to be introduced, we fill this position with the string #S#, which initiates derivations. We now allow the rules of the base to apply cyclically, preserving their linear order. Thus, for example, after having generated (24), with #S# in place of S', they reapply to the new occurrence of #S# in the terminal line of the derivation represented by (24). From this occurrence of #S# the rules of the base can generate the derivation represented by (25), with #S# in place of the occurrence of S' in (25). From the latter occurrence of #S#, the same base rules can reapply to form the derivation represented by (26). In this way, the base rules will generate the *generalized Phrase-marker* formed from (24), (25), (26) by replacing S' in (24) by (25) and replacing S' in (25) by (26).

We have thus revised the theory of the base by allowing # S # to appear on the right in certain branching rules, where previously the dummy symbol S' had appeared, and by allowing the rules to reapply (preserving their order) to these newly introduced occurrences of #S#. A generalized Phrase-marker formed in this way contains all of the base Phrase-markers that constitute the basis of a sentence, but it contains more information than a basis in the old sense since it also indicates explicity how these base Phrase-markers are embedded in one another. That is, the generalized Phrase-marker contains all of the information contained in the basis, as well as the information provided by the generalized embedding transformations.

In addition to the rules of the base, so modified, the grammar contains a linear sequence of singulary transformations. These apply to generalized Phrase-markers cyclically, in the following manner. First, the sequence of transformational rules applies to the most deeply embedded base Phrase-marker. (For example, it applies to (26), in the generalized Phrase-marker formed by embedding (26) in (25) and the result in (24), as described earlier.) Having applied to all such base Phrase-markers, the sequence of rules reapplies to a configuration dominated by S in which these base Phrase-markers are embedded (to (25), in the same example), and so on, until finally the sequence of rules applies to the configuration dominated by the initial symbol S of the entire generalized Phrase-marker (to (24), in our example). Notice that in the case of (24)–(26), the effect of this convention is precisely what is described in the Transformation-marker (28). That is, singulary transformations are applied to constituent sentences before they are embedded, and to matrix sentences after embedding has taken place. The embedding itself is now provided by the branching rules of the base rather than by generalized transformations. We have, in effect, converted the specific properties of the Transformation-marker (28) into general properties of any possible transformational derivation.

The grammar now consists of a base and a linear sequence of singulary transformations. These apply in the manner just described. The ordering possibilities that are permitted by the theory of Transformation-markers but apparently never put to use are now excluded in principle. The notion of Transformation-marker disappears, as does the notion of generalized transformation. The base rules form generalized Phrase-markers that contain just the information contained in the basis and the generalized transformations of the earlier version. But observe that in accordance with the Katz-Postal principle discussed earlier (p. 62), it is precisely this information that should be relevant to semantic interpretation. Consequently, we may take a generalized Phrase-marker, in the sense just defined, to be the deep structure generated by the syntactic component.

Thus the syntactic component consists of a base that generates deep structures and a transformational part that maps them into surface structures. The deep structure of a sentence is submitted to the semantic component for semantic interpretation, and its surface structure enters the phonological component and undergoes phonetic interpretation. The final effect of a grammar, then, is to relate a semantic interpretation to a phonetic representation—that is, to state how a sentence is interpreted. This relation is mediated by the syntactic component of the grammar, which constitutes its sole 'creative' part.

Such a description of the form of the syntactic component may seem strange if one considers the generative rules as a model for the actual construction of a sentence by a speaker. Thus it seems absurd to suppose that the speaker first forms a generalized Phrase-marker by base rules and then tests it for well-formedness by applying transformational rules to see if it gives, finally, a well-formed sentence. But this absurdity is simply a corollary to the deeper absurdity of regarding the system of generative rules as a point-by-point model for the actual construction of a sentence by a speaker. Consider the simpler case of a phrase structure grammar with no transformations (for example, the grammar of a programming language, or elementary arithmetic, or some small part of English that might be described in these terms). It would clearly be absurd to suppose that the 'speaker' of such a language, in formulating an 'utterance', first selects the major categories, then the categories into which these are analysed, and so forth, finally, at the end of the process, selecting the words or symbols that he is going to use (deciding what he is going to talk about). To think of a generative grammar in these terms is to take it to be a model of performance rather than a model of competence, thus totally misconceiving its nature. One can study models of performance that incorporate generative grammars, and some results have been achieved in such studies. But a generative grammar as it stands is no more a model of the speaker than it is a model of the hearer. Rather, as has been repeatedly emphasized, it can be regarded only as a characterization of the intrinsic tacit knowledge or competence that underlies actual performance.

The base rules and the transformational rules set certain conditions that must be met for a structure to qualify as the deep structure expressing the semantic content of some well-formed sentence. Given a grammar containing a base component and a transformational component, one can develop innumerable procedures for actually constructing deep structures. These will vary in exhaustiveness and efficiency, and in the extent to which they can be adapted to the problems of producing or understanding speech. One such constructive procedure is to run through the base rules (observing order) so as to form a generalized Phrase-marker M, and then through the transformational rules (observing order) so as to form a surface structure M' from M. If M' is well formed, then M was a deep structure; otherwise, it was not. All deep structures can be enumerated in this way, just as they can all be enumerated in many other ways, given the grammar. The grammar does not, in itself, provide any sensible procedure for finding the deep structure of a given sentence, or for producing a given sentence, just as it provides no sensible procedure for finding a paraphrase to a given sentence. It merely defines these tasks in a precise way. A performance model must certainly incorporate a grammar; it is not to be confused with a grammar. Once this point is clear, the fact that transformations act as a kind of filter will occasion no surprise or uneasiness.

To summarize, we have now suggested that the form of grammar may be as follows. A grammar contains a syntactic component, a semantic component, and a phonological component. The latter two are purely interpretative; they play no part in the recursive generation of sentence structures. The syntactic component consists of a base and a transformational component. The base, in turn, consists of a categorial subcomponent and a lexicon. The base generates deep structures. A deep structure enters the semantic component and receives a semantic interpretation; it is mapped by the transformational rules into a surface structure, which is then given a phonetic interpretation by the rules of the phonological component. Thus the grammar assigns semantic interpretations to signals, this association being mediated by the recursive rules of the syntactic component.

The categorial subcomponent of the base consists of a sequence of context-free rewriting rules. The function of these rules is, in essence, to define a certain system of grammatical relations that determine semantic interpretations, and to specify an abstract underlying order of elements that makes possible the functioning of the transformational rules. To a large extent, the rules of the base may be universal, and thus not, strictly speaking, part of particular grammars; or it may be that, although free in part, the choice of base rules is constrained by a universal condition on the grammatical functions that are defined. Similarly, the category symbols appearing in base rules are selected from a fixed universal alphabet; in fact, the choice of symbol may be largely or perhaps completely determined by the formal role the symbol plays in the system of base rules. The infinite generative capacity of the grammar arises from a particular formal property of these categorial rules, namely that they may introduce the initial symbol S into a line of a derivation. In this way, the rewriting rules can, in effect, insert base Phrase-markers into other base Phrase-markers, this process being iterable without limit.

The lexicon consists of an unordered set of lexical entries and certain redundancy rules. Each lexical entry is a set of features. Some of these are phonological features, drawn from a particular universal set of phonological features (the distinctive-feature system). The set of phonological features in a lexical entry can be extracted and represented as a phonological matrix that bears the relation 'is a' to each of the specified syntactic features belonging to the lexical entry. Some of the features are semantic features. These, too, are presumably drawn from a universal 'alphabet', but little is known about this today, and nothing has been said about it here. We call a feature 'semantic' if it is not mentioned in any syntactic rule, thus begging the question of whether semantics is involved in syntax. The redundancy rules of the lexicon add and specify features wherever this can be predicted by general rule. Thus the lexical entries constitute the full set of irregularities of the language.

We may construct a derivation of a generalized Phrase-marker by applying the categorial rules in the specified order, beginning with S, reapplying them to each new occurrence of S introduced in the course of the derivation. In this way, we derive a pre-terminal string, which becomes a generalized Phrase-marker when lexical entries are inserted in accordance with the transformational rules specified by the contextual features that belong to these lexical entries. The base of the syntactic component thus generates an infinite set of generalized Phrase-markers.

The transformational subcomponent consists of a sequence of singulary transformations. Each transformation is fully defined by a structure index, and a sequence of elementary transformations. Given a generalized Phrase-marker, we construct a transformational derivation by applying the sequence of transformational rules sequentially, 'from the bottom up'—that is, applying the sequence of rules to a given configuration only if we have already applied it to all base Phrase-markers embedded in this configuration. If none of the transformations blocks, we derive in this way a well-formed surface structure. In this and only this case, the generalized Phrase-marker to which the transformations were originally applied constitutes a deep structure, namely the deep structure of the sentence S, which is the terminal string of the derived surface structure. This deep structure expresses the semantic content of S, whereas the surface structure of S determines its phonetic form.

Aspects of the Theory of Syntax, 128–36, 139–43

4 Phonology

4.1 *Introductory*

[The main characteristics of generative phonology can be summarized as follows:

  it is part of an integrated theory of language;
  it is generative;
  it is mentalistic.

We will discuss these characteristics one by one in the following three sections.

A. *Generative phonology is part of an integrated theory of language*

To put it another way, generative phonology is not an autonomous level of linguistic description, but is dependent on information from other levels of the grammar, namely, surface structure and phonetics. It is important to realize that the dependency of phonology on other levels of description is not primarily a matter of descriptive convenience, but involves a claim about the nature of language. The validity of this claim cannot be fully discussed here, but we will attempt to illustrate some of the more important points with simple examples*.

(i) *The dependence of phonology on surface syntax*

This claim is based on empirical evidence and is not simply an act of faith or an *a priori* assumption. Thus, it is very often the case—and if we take a sufficiently abstract view of phonology it is probably always the case—that the morphemes of a language may be realized differently according to whether they appear in isolation or as part of a sentence, a nominal phrase, or some other syntactic category. To take a simple example from English, the [f] of the morpheme 'wife' is realized as [v] when 'wife' is combined with the plural morpheme to form a plural noun phrase (as in the phrase 'three wives'). However, the [f] of

---

* For a full discussion of this topic the reader is referred to Postal (1968).

'wife' does not always change across morpheme boundaries. For example, it does not change when 'wife' operates as part of a genitive noun phrase (as in 'my wife's handbag'). Furthermore, [f] never changes to [v] across word boundaries (cf. 'my wife is a teacher'). All languages show evidence for the dependence of sound structure on syntactic information, and it is for this reason that the rules of generative phonology operate on the output of the syntactic component of the grammar.

(ii) *The dependence of phonology on phonetics*

Before discussing the dependence of phonology on phonetics we must establish the nature of the difference between these two levels of linguistic description. Consider the following English words and their phonetic representations, where a raised 'h' expresses the fact that a consonant is 'aspirated', i.e. pronounced with a slight puff of air:

(1)   pit [p^{h}it]   spit [spit]
      tick [t^{h}ik]   stick [stik]
      kit [k^{h}it]   skit [skit]

It is evident that the sound properties represented by the symbol [s] serve to distinguish 'spit' from 'pit'. Similarly, [p] distinguishes 'pit' from 'bit' or 'spit' from 'skit'; [i] distinguishes 'pit' from 'pat' or 'put', and [t] distinguishes 'pit' from 'pick' or 'pill'. Since [s], [t], [p] and [i] serve to distinguish one word from another, we say that they have a contrastive value in the sound system of English. But consider now the sound property of aspiration as revealed by the data in (1). The fact that aspiration does not occur in words beginning with [s] leads us to suspect that aspiration is not a random phenomenon, and in fact a larger sample of data would show that the aspiration of initial consonants in English is perfectly regular under certain well-defined conditions. Since aspiration is regular and predictable in English, we conclude that it is non-contrastive, i.e. it cannot serve to distinguish one word from another. If aspiration were contrastive we might expect to find two words, say [pit] and [p^{h}it], which would be different in meaning. This is not the case in English, but aspiration is contrastive in some languages, for example, Hindi and Korean.

The difference between phonological and phonetic representations is illustrated by (2), where the slant lines and the square brackets are a convention to indicate phonological and phonetic statements respectively. Note that, since aspiration is non-contrastive in English, the raised 'h' does not appear in phonological representations.

(2)	phonological representation	phonetic representation
pit	/pit/	[pʰit]
spit	/spit/	[spit]
tick	/tik/	[tʰik]
stick	/stik/	[stik]
kit	/kit/	[kʰit]
skit	/skit/	[skit]

The task in generative phonology is to relate phonological and phonetic representations by means of a set of phonological rules (or 'laws') in such a way that the rules state explicitly what is predictable and what is non-predictable, or 'unique', in the sound system of a language. For example, under certain conditions the phonological process of aspiration shown in (1) and (2) is predictable and can be stated informally by means of the following rule:

(3) A voiceless stop consonant p, t or k is aspirated when followed immediately by a stressed vowel unless that consonant is immediately preceded by s.

Rule (3) states in a generalized form the fact that consonant aspiration in English is predictable under certain well-defined conditions. Thus if, in a given language, voiceless stops are never aspirated after /s/ but otherwise are always aspirated before a stressed vowel, these facts can be stated in the form of rules which apply to all strings generated by the grammar whenever the conditions stated by the rules are met. The aim of such rules is to eliminate from the phonological representation of morphemes all those 'redundant', or predictable, features which can be expressed in the form of generalized statements*. On the other hand, we must include in the phonological representation of morphemes all those sound properties which are not predictable by rule, but which are unique to a morpheme. Thus, the phonological representations of the morphemes in (2) were /pit/, /spit/, /tik/, /stik/, /kit/, and /skit/. This notation omits all reference to aspiration, which is predictable and can be handled by means of general rules, and represents only the unpredictable sound properties of the morphemes.

Let us return now to the question of why phonology must be dependent on phonetics. A partial answer to this question is implicit in the statement that phonological representations are abstractions from phonetic data. Clearly, if we say that B is abstracted from A we imply that B is dependent on A. However, the dependence claim for phonology involves a much more specific issue than the general 'abstractness principle'; it involves a condition known as the *naturalness relation* which is said to obtain between phonology and phonetics.

To exemplify, let us consider two sets of lexical items in English together with their phonological representations† :

(4)   *keep* /ki:p/, *kit* /kit/, *kate* /keit/,
        ken /kɛn/, *can* /kæn/

(5)   *cot* /kɔt/, *coat* /kout/, *coot* /ku:t/

In phonological terms the /k/s in both (4) and (5) are the same (i.e. they 'belong to the same phoneme') but phonetically the /k/ in (4) (which we might call [k]₁) is quite different from the /k/ in (5): [k]₂. We say that [k]₁ and [k]₂ are allophones of the same phoneme. The difference between the two allophones of /k/ lies in the fact that [k]₁ is articulated much further forward in the mouth than [k]₂. This phenomenon is known as *fronting*. The fronting of /k/ under the

* Hence the name lexical redundancy rules ('morpheme structure rules' in the older terminology). [A, B]

† These phonological representations are only approximate, but this does not affect our argument. [A, B]

condition obtaining in (5) is predictable, and can be stated in the form
of a rule:

(6)

$$[k] \longrightarrow \begin{bmatrix} k \\ + \end{bmatrix} / \underline{\hspace{1cm}} \begin{Bmatrix} i: \\ i \\ ei \\ \varepsilon \\ æ \end{Bmatrix}$$

that is to say, '/k/ is realized as [k̟] before the vowels /i:, i, ei, ε, æ/.
Notice that, indirectly, rule (6) states that /k/ is not realized as [k̟]
before the vowels /ɔ, ou, u:/.

Rule (6) describes the phenomenon of fronting without explaining
it. However, Chomsky's requirement that a theory of language should
attain the level of explanatory adequacy prompts us to ask the following question. *Why* is /k/ fronted in some environments but not in others
and how do we incorporate the answer, if any, into our linguistic
theory? There are three possible answers to questions of this sort,
and they have all been given at different times in the past, though
perhaps not to this particular question.

(i) The question is invalid because in phonology we do not want
to explain but to describe.

(ii) Fronting, together with all other phonological processes, is
random and cannot be explained.

(iii) The vowels /i:, i, ei, ε, æ/ have something in common phonetically which causes fronting (and, by implication, /ɔ, ou, u:/
have something in common which prevents fronting).

The first answer is difficult to justify on general philosophical grounds,
for it is surely the task of any theory not only to describe but also to
explain phenomena, i.e. to attain the level of explanatory adequacy.
The second answer is the one which is implicit in rule (6). The interpretation of rule (6) is that the vowels in the list have no feature in
common which can be said to cause the fronting of /k/. In other
words, it is implied that the fronting of /k/ is a random phonological
process, and it is a matter of mere chance that the list contains, for
example, no back vowels.

But this conclusion seems to be intuitively wrong. Any phonetician
knows that the vowels listed in rule (6) have something in common,
namely, their 'frontness' and is prepared to accept the hypothesis
that it is this feature which causes the fronting of /k/. The fact that

rule (6) fails to state explicitly what it is that all the vowels have in
common in order to cause the fronting of /k/ is evidently a weakness
in rules of this type, which are very common in non-generative
phonologies.

If we want to assert the fact that the vowels /iː, i, ei, ɛ, æ/ possess
the property of 'frontness' as a common feature, and that it is precisely
this property that causes the fronting of /k/, we can do so by means of
the following rule, where /k/ is an abbreviation for a set of features:

$$(7) \quad /k/ \longrightarrow [+\text{front}] \Big/ \underline{\quad\quad} \begin{bmatrix} +\text{vowel} \\ +\text{front} \end{bmatrix}$$

(Read: '/k/ is fronted whenever it occurs before a front vowel'.)
Rule (7), unlike rule (6), abstracts the phonetic properties [+front]
and [+vowel] which the list of sounds /iː, i, ei, ɛ, æ/ have in common,
and presents this property as a *necessary condition* for the fronting of /k/,
and presents this property as a *necessary condition* for the fronting of /k/.
Thus it is no longer a matter of mere chance, but a matter of principle,
that the list of sounds in rule (7) contains no back vowels. Note that
rule (7) sets up a necessary condition for the fronting of /k/, but it
does not, in itself, explain the fact that only front vowels condition
fronting. In order to explain the process of fronting we would have to
go outside phonology and have recourse to phonetic theory, where we
might seek an explanation in terms of 'ease of articulation', for example.

If we assume that phonological processes are non-random, and that
we can state them in the form of rules which utilize phonetic properties
such as [+front], [+vowel], it follows that an explanatorily adequate
theory must be constructed on the basis of a set of all those phonetic
parameters, or 'distinctive features', which are relevant to the formulation of the phonological rules. Accordingly, Chomsky uses a 'universal
phonetic alphabet' of distinctive features to represent those phonetic
parameters which are relevant to his theory, and Chomsky's phonology
is therefore dependent on phonetics in this strong sense. In other
words, there is a 'naturalness' condition between generative phonology
and phonetics as a consequence of the fact that many phonological
processes are 'natural' (i.e. non-random and explainable in terms of
properties that have been established by phonetic theory).

It might be asked whether all phonological processes are 'natural'
in the sense just described. The answer to this question depends on
the current state of phonetic theory. To illustrate let us suppose,

contrary to fact, that phonetic theory does not specify the set of vowels /iː, i, ei, ɛ, æ/ as front vowels, and that this set does not constitute a natural class. Given this situation, we might feel obliged to characterize the process of fronting as random. A more fruitful approach, however, would be to act upon the strong hypothesis that fronting is not random and to assume that the vowels which condition fronting must have some phonetic parameter in common. At this point the burden of responsibility is passed back to the phonetician in the hope that he will be able to set up an additional distinctive feature which will enable the phonologist to state the condition for fronting in terms of a 'natural' class.

It becomes clear, therefore, that there is a mutual dependence relation between phonetics and generative phonology. Phonological rules must be expressed in terms of parameters established by phonetic theory, but problems of description at the phonological level may lead in their turn to a modification of phonetic theory. In this way the 12 distinctive features originally specified by Jakobson, Fant and Halle (1951) have steadily increased in number, until at the present moment a set of about 28 distinctive features serves as the explanatory basis for generative phonology. The heuristic strategy of acting on strong hypotheses concerning explanatory adequacy is a marked characteristic of generative phonology, and it is this which has led to a recent renewal of interest in phonetic theory*.

B. *The 'generativeness' of generative phonology*

Chomsky points out that it is the task of the phonological component 'to map phonological representations onto phonetic representations'. That is, given a syntactic string which consists of the phonological representations of lexical morphemes (together with grammatical morphemes such as 'plural') the application of certain phonological rules will, if the rules are explicit, automatically convert this string into a string of phonetic representations. In short, the rules *generate* the phonetic representation of the sentence.

Four basic ingredients are necessary to generate the phonetic representation of a sentence:

(1)   The unique sound properties of the morphemes. These are represented in the lexicon—hence the term 'lexical representation'.
(2)   The syntactic organization of morphemes in surface structure.

* See Postal (1968), Chomsky and Halle (1968).

(3)   Those redundancy rules which specify the predictable sound properties of the individual morphemes.

(4)   Those phonological rules which specify sound properties (stress, for example) of parts of the sentence (noun phrases, verb phrases, etc.) and ultimately of the whole sentence.

It is the task of the phonologist to describe in maximally general terms how these basic ingredients are manifested in individual languages using a formal descriptive apparatus which applies to *all* languages (i.e. universally).

As we have seen, it is one of the basic tenets of generative phonology as currently practised that phonetic parameters, or distinctive features, should form part of the universal apparatus of linguistic description if phonological processes are to be adequately described*. One consequence of this requirement is that both phonological rules and lexical representations must be formulated in terms of distinctive features rather than in terms of segmental phonemes, as in 'neo-Bloomfieldian' phonology. For example, rather than formulate our fronting rule as in (8) it is considered preferable to generalize the rule by using 'matrices' of distinctive features, as in (9):

(8)
$$
\begin{Bmatrix} k \\ g \end{Bmatrix} \longrightarrow \begin{Bmatrix} k \\ + \\ g \\ + \end{Bmatrix} \Big/ \underline{\quad} \begin{Bmatrix} i: \\ i \\ ei \\ \varepsilon \\ \text{æ} \end{Bmatrix}
$$

---

* Note that although distinctive feature theory has been incorporated in a specific way in generative phonology, it existed prior to generative phonology and is logically independent of it. The advantages of (7) over (6) were stressed, in a different notation and general framework of thinking, by Jakobson and the Prague linguists, among others. The use of distinctive feature theory and the reinterpretation of the theory in order to permit the necessary abstractness made an important contribution to the development of generative phonology, but it is nevertheless the case that matters like the relation of (6) and (7) are the basic issues for distinctive feature theory, while questions of ordering and organization of rules, abstractness of phonological representation and the like are the kind that are handled by generative phonology. When distinctive feature theory and generative phonology come together we have the kind of system that is found in the work of Chomsky and Halle. [A, B]

$$(9) \quad \begin{bmatrix} +\text{stop} \\ +\text{back} \end{bmatrix} \longrightarrow \begin{bmatrix} +\text{prevelar} \end{bmatrix} \Big/ \underline{\quad} \begin{bmatrix} +\text{vowel} \\ +\text{front} \end{bmatrix} *$$

Notice that rule (9) correctly implies that it is irrelevant to the process of fronting whether the back consonant is voiced [g] or voiceless [k]. In other words rule (8), as a result of using lists of segmental phonemes, contains both too much and too little information (too much because it distinguishes voiced and voiceless consonants, too little because it does not give the phonetic parameters which these consonants have in common). Rule (9) is valued more highly than rule (8) because it contains fewer symbols *and* expresses a 'linguistically significant generalization'†.

The use of phonetic parameters in phonological rules naturally entails their use in lexical representations. Hence the fact, which Chomsky refers to in passing, that the lexical entry of a morpheme in the lexicon of a generative grammar appears as a matrix of distinctive features which are unique to that morpheme (Chomsky refers to them as 'classificatory matrices'). For example, using the (simplified) features of rule (9), the morpheme 'keep' might appear in the lexicon as (10), where the three columns represent the phonemes /k/, /i:/ and /p/ respectively:

$$(10) \quad 1 \qquad\qquad\qquad 2 \qquad\qquad\qquad 3$$

$$\begin{bmatrix} +\text{stop} \\ +\text{voiceless} \\ +\text{back} \end{bmatrix} \qquad \begin{bmatrix} +\text{front} \\ +\text{high} \\ +\text{long} \end{bmatrix} \qquad \begin{bmatrix} +\text{stop} \\ +\text{voiceless} \\ +\text{bilabial} \end{bmatrix}$$

The phonological process of fronting would then apply by virtue of the fact that the lexical representation of 'keep' incorporates the relevant

---

* The feature [+ prevelar] indicates an articulation which involves both the velar region (i.e. the 'back' region) and the palatal region of the mouth cavity. For simplicity, we use features of our own which do not appear in distinctive feature theory. For a full account of distinctive feature theory see Jakobson, Fant and Halle (1951), Halle (1962), Chomsky and Halle (1968). [A, B]

† An explanatorily adequate theory must contain an evaluation procedure that selects the most highly valued hypothesis from a set of hypotheses of the appropriate form, each of which meets a condition of compatibility with the data. For a full discussion of the role of an evaluation procedure or 'simplicity metric' in generative phonology, see Chomsky and Halle (1968), Chapter 8. [A, B]

features $\begin{bmatrix} +\text{stop} \\ +\text{back} \end{bmatrix}$ in the first column plus the relevant feature

[+front], which follows immediately in the second column.

Another important aspect of generative phonology is the fact that the phonological rules may delete, add and permute elements during the process of generating a sentence. In the fronting rule (9), for example, the feature [+back] is deleted and a new feature [+prevelar] added. The changes involved in this particular example are of a very simple nature but in many cases the successive application of rules, each one simple in itself, may mean that there is a striking difference between the phonological and the phonetic representations. The use of 'transformational' rules is a direct result of the phonologist's search for 'laws' of ever-increasing generality. A notable example occurs on page 97 where Chomsky postulates an underlying velar fricative—as in the Scottish word *loch*—for English although this is never realized phonetically in present-day standard English. (Velar fricatives occurred phonetically in Middle English and do also in certain modern dialects of English.)

C. *The mentalistic character of generative phonology*

Chomsky's concept of 'mentalism' has often been misrepresented, and it is therefore important to emphasize that the mentalistic character of generative linguistics is vital from Chomsky's point of view. The concept of mentalism, despite the rather misleading label with its connotations of introspection and unfalsifiability, is in fact quite simple. As we have pointed out at the beginning of this book, a mentalistic approach to language means that a linguistic theory is regarded as a partial theory of the human mind and that human beings, as the actual possessors of language in all its aspects, should form the explanatory and empirical domain of linguistic theory. In particular, Chomsky claims that no principled decision about the validity of linguistic descriptions can be made unless linguistic theory is regarded as part of a theory of mind. In other words, linguistic theories which have no mentalistic basis must ultimately be arbitrary because they are non-explanatory. It follows that the two concepts of mentalism and explanatory adequacy are two sides of the same coin, and that a linguistic theory should both describe and explain a speaker's linguistic competence.

The mentalistic counterparts of linguistic descriptions are by no means transparent, and it is the task of the linguist to show that these counterparts exist. Let us take one more example from phonology to illustrate this point. It was said above (p. 71) that consonant aspiration in English is generally predictable and that therefore it need not be stated in phonological or lexical representations. However, it could conceivably be argued that some features of aspiration should be represented at the phonological level. What criteria can be adduced for choosing one alternative rather than the other? The answer to this question is linked to the requirement that linguistics should have a mentalistic basis.

Our discussion about predictable and non-predictable phenomena implied the existence of two different types of linguistic knowledge, which we may term 'ad hoc' and 'systematic' knowledge. For example, an English speaker's knowledge that the name for a writing instrument consists of three phonemes /p/, /ɛ/, /n/ is ad hoc knowledge (it might just as well have been /m/, /i/, /k/, or any other sequence of phonemes), whereas his knowledge that the /p/ in /pɛn/ is aspirated, is systematic and has nothing to do with the unique qualities of the morpheme. A simple way of testing this would be to write down the orthographic nonsense syllable 'tek' and ask a native speaker to pronounce it. It is safe to say that no native speaker would show any hesitation in aspirating the /t/ even though he had never heard the word before. Chomsky claims that this distinction between the two types of linguistic knowledge is captured by the difference between phonological representations and phonological rules. The former should be a representation of the speaker's unique knowledge, and the latter should be a representation of his systematic knowledge. Thus it is claimed that generative phonology, unlike non-mentalistic phonologies, can give a principled answer to the question whether predictable properties should or should not be stated in lexical representations. It is Chomsky's view that links of this kind between linguistic phenomena and mental processes should be established at every stage of linguistic description. [A, B]]

4.2 *The role of the phonological component*

We regard a grammar as having two fundamental components, a *syntactic component* of the kind we have already described and a *phonological component* to which we now briefly turn our attention.

The syntactic component of a grammar contains rewriting rules and transformational rules and it gives as its output terminal strings with structural descriptions. The structural description of a terminal string contains, in particular, a *derived P-marker* that assigns to this string a labelled bracketing; in the present section we consider only this aspect of the structural description. We therefore limit attention to such items as the following, taken (with many details omitted) as an example of the output of the syntactic component:

(11) $[_S[_{NP}[_N \#\text{Ted} \#]_N]_{NP}[_{VP}[_V \#\text{see}]_V$ past $\#$
          $[_{NP}[_{Det} \# \text{ the dem pl} \#]_{Det} [_N \#\text{book}]_N$ pl $\#]_{NP}]_{VP}]_S$,

(where the symbol $\#$ is used to indicate the word boundaries)*. The terminal string, (11), is a representation of the sentence *Ted saw those books*, which we might represent on the phonetic level in the following manner:

(12) $\overset{1}{\text{t}^\text{h}\text{e·d}} + \overset{2}{\text{sɔw}} + \overset{3}{\text{ðəwz}} + \overset{1}{\text{buks}}$,

(where the numerals indicate stress level) again omitting many refinements, details, discussions of alternatives, and many phonetic features to which we pay no attention in these brief remarks.

Representations such as (12) identify an utterance in a rather direct manner. We can assume that these representations are given in terms of a *universal phonetic system* which consists of a phonetic alphabet and a set of general phonetic laws. The symbols of the phonetic alphabet are defined in physical (i.e. acoustic and articulatory) terms; the general laws of the universal phonetic system deal with the manner in which physical items represented by these symbols may combine in a natural language. The universal phonetic system is a part of general linguistic theory rather than a specific part of the grammar of a particular language. Just as in the case of the other aspects of the general theory of linguistic structure, a particular formulation of the universal phonetic system represents a hypothesis about linguistic universals and can be regarded as a hypothesis concerning some of the innate data-processing and concept-forming capacities that a child brings to bear in language learning.

The role of the phonological component of a generative grammar is to relate representations such as (11) and (12); that is to say, the phonological component embodies those processes that determine the

---

* This labelled bracketing is a notational variant of the more familiar tree-diagram, see page 25. [A, B]

phonetic shape of an utterance, given the morphemic content and general syntactic structure of this utterance, (as in (11)). As distinct from the syntactic component, it plays no part in the formulation of new utterances but merely assigns to them a phonetic shape. Although investigation of the phonological component does not, therefore, properly form a part of the study of mathematical models for linguistic structure, the processes by which phonetic shape is assigned to utterances have a great deal of independent interest. We shall indicate briefly some of their major features.

4.3 *Phones and phonemes*

The phonological component can be thought of as an input-output device that accepts a terminal string with a labelled bracketing and codes it as a phonetic representation. The phonetic representation is a sequence of symbols of the phonetic alphabet, some of which (e.g. the first three of (12)) are directly associated with physically defined features, others (e.g. the symbol + in (12)), with features of transition. Let us call the first kind *phonetic segments* and the second kind *phonetic junctures*. Let us consider more carefully the character of the phonetic segments.

Each symbol of the universal phonetic alphabet is an abbreviation of a certain set of physical features. For example, the symbol [p^h] represents a labial aspirated unvoiced stop. These symbols have no independent status in themselves; they merely serve as notational abbreviations. Consequently a representation such as (12), and, in general, any phonetic representation, can be most appropriately regarded as a *phonetic matrix*: the rows represent the physical properties that are considered primitive in the linguistic theory in question and the columns stand for successive segments of the utterance (aside from junctures). The matrix element (i,j) indicates whether (or to what degree) the jth segment has the ith property. The phonetic segments thus correspond to columns of a matrix. In (12) the symbol [$\frac{3}{3}$] might be an abbreviation for the column [vocalic, nonconsonantal, grave, compact, unrounded, voiced, lax, tertiary stress, etc.], assuming a universal phonetic theory based on features that have been proposed by Jakobson as constituting a universal phonetic system. Matrices with such entries constitute the output of the phonological component of the grammar.

What is the input to the phonological component? The terminal string (11) consists of *lexical morphemes*, such as *Ted, book*; *grammatical morphemes*, such as *past, plural*; and certain *junctural elements*, such as #. The junctural elements are introduced by rules of the syntactic component in order to indicate positions in which morphological and syntactic structures have phonetic effects. They can, in fact, be regarded as grammatical morphemes for our purposes. Each grammatical morpheme is in general, represented by a single terminal symbol, unanalysed into features. On the other hand, the lexical morphemes are represented rather by strings of symbols that we call *phonemic segments* or simply *phonemes**. Aside from the labelled brackets, then, the input to the phonological component is a string consisting of phonemes and special symbols for grammatical morphemes. The representation in (11) is essentially accurate, except for the fact that lexical morphemes are given in ordinary orthography instead of in phonemic notation. Thus, *Ted, see, the, book*, should be replaced by /ted/, /sī/, /ðī/, /buk/, respectively. We have, of course, given so little detail in (12) that phonetic and phonemic segments are scarcely distinguished in this example.

We shall return shortly to the question: What is the relation between phonemic and phonetic segments? Observe for now that there is no requirement so far that they be closely related.

Before going on to consider the status of the phonemic segments more carefully, we should like to warn the reader that there is considerable divergence of usage with regard to the terms phoneme, phonetic representation, etc., in the linguistic literature. Furthermore, that divergence is not merely terminological; it reflects deep-seated differences of opinion, far from resolved today, regarding the real nature of sound structure. In the present discussion our underlying conceptions of sound structure are close to those of the founders of modern phonology but diverge quite sharply from the position that has been more familiar during the last twenty years, particularly in the United States—a position that is often called neo-Bloomfieldian. In particular, our present usage of the term phoneme is much like that of Sapir (e.g. Sapir, 1933), and our notion of a universal phonetic system has its roots in such classical work as Sweet (1877) and de Saussure (1916—the Appendix to the Introduction, which dates, in fact, from 1897). What we, following Sapir, call phonemic representation is generally

* More precisely, we should take the phonemes to be the segments that appear at the stage of derivation at which all grammatical morphemes have been eliminated by the phonological rules. [C]

called morphophonemic today. It is generally assumed that there is a level of representation intermediate between phonetic and morphophonemic, this new intermediate level usually being called phonemic. However, there seems to us good reason to reject the hypothesis that there exists an intermediate level of this sort and to reject, as well, many of the assumptions concerning sound structure that are closely interwoven with this hypothesis in many contemporary formulations of linguistic theory.

Clearly, we should attempt to discover general rules that apply to such large classes of elements as consonants, stops, voiced segments, etc., rather than to individual elements. We should, in short, try to replace a mass of separate observations by simple generalizations. Since the rules will apply to classes of elements, elements must be identified as members of certain classes. Thus each phoneme will belong to several overlapping categories in terms of which the phonological rules are stated. In fact, we can represent each phoneme simply by the set of categories to which it belongs; in other words, we can represent each lexical item by a *classificatory matrix* in which columns stand for phonemes and rows for categories and the entry (i,j) indicates whether or not phoneme j belongs to category i. Each phoneme is now represented as a sequence of categories, which we can call *distinctive features*, using one of the current senses of this term. Like the phonetic symbols, the phonemes have no independent status in themselves. It is an extremely important and by no means obvious fact that the distinctive features of the classificatory phonemic matrix define categories that correspond closely to those determined by the rows of the phonetic matrices. This point was noted by Sapir (1925) and has been elaborated in recent years by Jakobson, Fant, and Halle (1951) and by Jakobson and Halle (1956); it is an insight that has its roots in the classical linguistics that flourished in India more than two millenia ago.

4.4 *Invariance and linearity conditions*

The input to the phonological component thus consists, in part, of distinctive-feature matrices representing lexical items; and the output consists of phonetic matrices (and phonetic junctures). What is to be the relation between the categorial, distinctive-feature matrix that constitutes the input and the corresponding phonetic matrix that results from application of the phonological rules? What is to be the relation, for example, between the input matrix abbreviated as /ted/

(where each of the symbols /t/, /e/, /d/ stands for a column containing a plus in a given row if the symbol in question belongs to the category associated with that row, a minus if the symbol is specified as not belonging to this category, and a blank if the symbol is unspecified with respect to membership in this category) and the output matrix abbreviated as [tʰė·d] (where each of the symbols [tʰ], [ė·], [d] stands for a column, the entries of which indicate phonetic properties)?

The strongest requirement that could be imposed would be that the input classificatory matrix must literally be a submatrix of the output phonetic matrix, differing from it only by the deletion of certain redundant entries. Thus the phonological rules would fill in the blanks of the classificatory matrix to form the corresponding phonetic matrix. This strong condition, for example, is required by Jakobson and, implicitly, by Bloch in their formulations of phonemic theory*. If this condition is met, then phonemic representation will satisfy what we can call the invariance condition and the linearity condition.

By the *linearity condition* we refer to the requirement that each phoneme must have associated with it a particular stretch of sound in the represented utterance and that, if phoneme A is to the left of phoneme B in the phonemic representation, the stretch associated with A precedes the stretch associated with B in the physical event. (We are limiting ourselves here to what are called *segmental phonemes*, since we are regarding the so-called supra-segmentals as features of them.)

The *invariance condition* requires that to each phoneme A there be associated a certain defining set $\Sigma(A)$ of physical phonetic features, such that each variant (allophone) of A has all the features of $\Sigma(A)$, and no phonetic segment which is not a variant (allophone) of A has all of the features of $\Sigma(A)$.

If both the invariance and linearity conditions were met, the task of building machines capable of recognizing the various phonemes in normal human speech would be greatly simplified. Correctness of these conditions would also suggest a model of perception based on segmentation and classification and would lend support to the view that the methods of analysis required in linguistics should be limited to segmentation and classification. However, correctness of these requirements

---

* They would not regard what they call phonemic representations as the input to the phonological component. However, as previously mentioned, we see no way of maintaining the view that there is an intermediate representation of the type called 'phonemic' by these and other phonologists. [C]

is a question of fact, not of decision, and it seems to us that there are strong reasons to doubt that they are correct. Therefore, we shall not assume that for each phoneme there must be some set of phonetic properties that uniquely identifies all of its variants and that these sets literally occur in a temporal sequence corresponding to the linear order of phonemes.

We cannot go into the question in detail, but a single example may illustrate the kind of difficulty that leads us to reject the linearity and invariance conditions. Clearly the English words *write* and *ride* must appear in any reasonable phonemic representation as /rayt/ and /rayd/, respectively—that is, they differ phonemically in the voicing of the final consonant. They differ phonetically in the vowel also. Consider, for example, a dialect in which *write* is phonetically [rayt] and *ride* is phonetically [ra·yd], with the characteristic automatic lengthening before voiced consonants. To derive the phonetic from the phonemic representation in this case, we apply the phonetic rule,

(13)   vowels become lengthened before voiced segments,

which is quite general and can easily be incorporated into our present framework. Consider now the words *writer* and *rider* in such a dialect. Clearly, the syntactic component will indicate that *writer* is simply *write* + agent and *rider* is simply *ride* + agent, where the lexical entries *write* and *ride* are exactly as given; that is, we have the phonemic representations /rayt +r/, /rayd + r/ for *writer*, *rider*, respectively. However, there is a rather general rule (in American English) that the phonemes /t/ and /d/ merge in an alveolar flap [D] in several contexts, in particular, after main stress as in *writer* and *rider*. Thus the grammar for this dialect may contain the phonetic rule,

(14)   [t, d]→D after main stress.

Applying Rules (13) and (14), *in this order*, to the phonemic representations /rayt+r/, /rayd+r/, we derive first [rayt+r], [ra·yd+r], by Rule (13), and eventually [rayDr], [ra·yDr], by Rule (14), as the phonetic representations of the words *writer*, *rider*. Note, however, that the phonemic representations of these words differ only in the *fourth* segment (voiced consonant versus unvoiced consonant), whereas the phonetic representations differ only in the *second* segment (longer vowel versus shorter vowel). Consequently, it seems impossible to maintain that a sequence of phonemes $A_1 \ldots A_m$ is associated with the sequence of phonetic segments $a_1 \ldots a_m$, where a_i contains the set of features that uniquely identify A_i in addition to certain redundant features. This is a typical example that shows the untenability of the linearity and invariance conditions for phonemic representation. It follows that phonemes cannot be derived from phonetic representations by simple procedures of segmentation and classification by criterial attributes, at least as these are ordinarily construed.

Notice, incidentally, that we have nowhere specified that the phonetic features constituting the universal system must be defined in absolute terms. Thus one of the universal features might be the feature 'front versus back' or 'short versus long'. If a phonetic segment A differs from a phonetic segment B only in that A has the feature 'short' whereas B has the feature 'long', this means that in any particular context $X—Y$ the longer element is identified as B and the shorter as A. It may be that A in one context is actually as long as or longer than B in another context. Many linguists, however, have required that phonetic features must be defined in absolute terms. Instead of the feature 'short versus long', they require us to identify the absolute length (to some approximation) of each segment. If we add this requirement to the invariance condition, we conclude that even partial overlapping of phonemes—that is, assignment of a phone a to a phoneme B in one context and to the phoneme C in a different context, in which the choice is contextually determined—cannot be tolerated. Such, apparently, is the view of Bloch (1948, 1950). This is an extremely restrictive assumption which is invalidated not only by such examples as the one we have just given but by a much wider range of examples of partial overlapping (see Bloch, 1940, for examples). In fact, work in acoustic phonetics (Liberman, Delattre, and Cooper, 1952; Schatz, 1954) has shown that if this condition must be met, where features are defined in auditory and acoustic terms (as proposed in Bloch, 1950), then not even the analysis of the stops /p, t, k/ can be maintained, since they overlap, a consequence that is surely a reduction to absurdity.

The requirements of relative or of absolute invariance both suggest models for speech perception, but the difficulty (or impossibility) of maintaining either of these requirements suggests that these models are incorrect and leads to alternative proposals of a kind to which we shall return.

We return now to the main theme.

4.5 *Cyclic ordering of phonological rules*

We have described the input to the phonological component of the grammar as a terminal string consisting of lexical morphemes, grammatical morphemes, and junctures, with the constituent structure marked. This component gives as its output a phonetic matrix in which the columns stand for successive segments and the rows for phonetic features. Obviously, we want the rules of the phonological component to be as few and general as possible. In particular, we prefer rules that apply to large and to natural classes of elements and that have a simple and brief specification of relevant context. We prefer a set of rules in which the same classes of elements figure many times. These and other requirements are met if we define the complexity of the phonological component in terms of the number of features mentioned in the rules, where the form of rules is specified in such a way as to facilitate valid generalizations (Halle, 1961). We then choose simpler (more general) grammars over more complex ones with more feature specifications (more special cases).

The problem of phonemic analysis is to assign to each utterance a phonemic representation, consisting of matrices in which the columns stand for phonemes and the rows for distinctive (classificatory) features, and to discover the simplest set of rules (where simplicity is a well-defined formal notion) that determine the phonetic matrices corresponding to given phonemic representations. There is no general requirement that the linearity and invariance conditions will be met by phonemic representations. It is therefore an interesting and important observation that these conditions are, in fact, substantially met, although there is an important class of exceptions.

In order to determine a phonetic representation, the phonological rules must utilize other information outside the phonemic representation; in particular, they must utilize information about its constituent structure. Consequently, it is in general impossible for a linguist (or a child learning the language) to discover the correct phonemic representation without an essential use of syntactic information. Similarly, it would be expected that in general the perceiver of speech should utilize syntactic cues in determining the phonemic representation of a presented utterance—he should, in part, base his identification of the utterance on his partial understanding of it, a conclusion that is not at all paradoxical.

The phonological component consists of (1) a sequence of rewriting rules, including, in particular, a subsequence of *morpheme structure rules*, (2) a sequence of *transformational rules*, and (3) a sequence of rewriting rules that we can call *phonetic rules*. They are applied to a terminal string in the order given.

7

Morpheme structure rules enable us to simplify the matrices that specify the individual lexical morphemes by taking advantage of general properties of the whole set of matrices. In English, for example, if none of the three initial segments of a lexical item is a vowel, the first must be /s/, the second a stop, and the third a liquid or glide. This information need not therefore be specified in the matrices that represent such morphemes as *string* and *square*. Similarly, the glide ending an initial consonant cluster need not be further specified, since it is determined by the following vowel; except after /s/, it is /y/ if followed by /u/, and it is /w/ otherwise. Thus we have *cure* and *queer* but not /kwūr/ or /kyīr/. There are many other rules of this sort. They permit us to reduce the number of features mentioned in the grammar, since one morpheme structure rule may apply to many matrices, and they thus contribute to simplicity, as previously defined.

Transformational phonemic rules determine the phonetic effects of constituent structure. (Recall that the fundamental feature of transformational rules, as they have been defined, is that they apply to a string by virtue of the fact that it has a particular constituent structure.) In English there is a complex interplay of rules of stress assignment and vowel reduction that leads to a phonetic output with many degrees of stress and an intricate distribution of reduced and unreduced vowels. These rules involve constituent structure in an essential manner at both the morphological and the syntactic level; consequently, they must be classified as transformational rather than rewriting rules. They are ordered, and apply in a *cycle*, first to the smallest constituents (that is, lexical morphemes), then to the next larger ones, and so on, until the largest domain of phonetic processes is reached. It is a striking fact, in English at least, that essentially the same rules apply both inside and outside the word. Thus we have only a single cycle of transformational rules, which, by repeated application, determines the phonetic form of isolated words as well as of complex phrases. The cyclic ordering of these rules, in effect, determines the phonetic structure of a complex form, whether morphological or syntactic, in terms of the phonetic structure of its underlying elements.

The rules of stress assignment and vowel reduction are the basic elements of the transformational cycle in English. Placement of main stress is determined by constituent type and final affix. As main stress is placed in a certain position, all other stresses in the construction are automatically weakened. Continued reapplication of this rule to successively larger constituents of a string with no original stress indications can thus lead to an output with a many-levelled stress contour. A vowel is reduced to [ɨ] in certain phonemic positions if it has never received main stress at an earlier stage of the derivation or if successive cycles have weakened its original main stress to tertiary (or, in certain positions, to secondary). The rule of vowel reduction applies only once in the transformational cycle, namely, when we reach the level of the word.

A detailed discussion of these rules is not feasible within the limits of this chapter, but a few comments may indicate how they operate. Consider in particular, the following four rules*, which apply in the order given:

(15a)   A *substantive* rule that assigns stress in initial position in nouns (also stems) under very general circumstances.

(15b)   A *nuclear stress* rule that makes the last main stress dominant, thus weakening all other stresses in the construction.

(15c)   The *vowel reduction* rule.

(15d)   A rule of *stress adjustment* that weakens all nonmain stresses in a word by one.

From the verbs *permít, tormént*, etc., we derive the nouns *pérmit, tórment* in the next transformational cycle by the substantive rule, the stress on the second syllable being automatically weakened to secondary. The rule of stress adjustment gives primary-tertiary as the stress sequence in these cases. The second syllable does not reduce to [ɨ], since it is protected by secondary stress at the stage at which the rule of vowel-reduction applies.

Thus for *pérmit, tórment* we have the following derivations:

1. $[_N[_V \text{ per} + \text{mit}]_V]_N$ $[_N[_V \text{ torment}]_V]_N$

2. $[_N[_V \text{ per} + \overset{1}{\text{mit}}]_V]_N$ $[_N[_V \text{ torment}]_V]_N$

3. $[_N \text{ per} + \overset{1}{\text{mit}}]_N$ $[_N \overset{1}{\text{torment}}]_N$

4. $[_N \overset{1}{\text{per}} + \overset{2}{\text{mit}}]_N$ $[_N \overset{1}{\text{torment}}]_N$

5. $\overset{1}{\text{per}} + \overset{2}{\text{mit}}$ $\overset{1}{\text{torment}}$

6. $\overset{1}{\text{per}} + \overset{3}{\text{mit}}$ $\overset{1}{\text{torment}}$

7. $\overset{1}{\text{p}}^{\text{h}}\overset{3}{\text{ɨrmit}}$ $\text{t}^{\text{h}}\overset{1}{\text{ɔ}}\overset{3}{\text{rment}}$

---

* These differ somewhat from the rules that would appear in a more detailed and general grammar. See Chomsky and Halle (1968) for details. [C]

Line 1 is the phonemic, line 7 the phonetic representation (details omitted). Line 2 is derived by a general rule (that we have not given) for *torment* and by Rule (15b) for *permit* (since the heaviest stress in this case is zero). Line 3 terminates the first transformational cycle by erasing innermost brackets. Line 4 results from Rule (15a). Line 5 terminates the second transformational cycle, erasing innermost brackets. Line 6 results from Rule (15d) ((15c) being inapplicable because of secondary stress on the second vowel), and line 7 results from other phonetic rules.

Consider, in contrast, the word *torrent*. This, like *torment*, has phonemic /e/ as its second vowel (cf. *torrential*), but it is not, like *tórment*, derived from a verb *torrént*. Consequently, the second vowel does not receive main stress on the first cycle; it will therefore reduce by Rule (15c) to [ɨ]. Thus we have reduced and unreduced vowels contrasting in *tórment-tórrent* as a result of a difference in syntactic analysis. Initial stress in *tórrent* is again a result of Rule (15a).

The same rule that forms *pérmit* and *tórment* from *permít* and *tormént* changes the secondary stress of the final syllable of the verb *advocate* to tertiary, so that it is reduced to [ɨ] by the rule of vowel reduction (15c). Thus we have reduced and unreduced vowels contrasting in the noun *advocate* and the verb *advocate* and generally with the suffix *-ate*. Exactly the same rules give the contrast between reduced and unreduced vowels in the noun *compliment* ([. . . mɨnt]) and the verb *compliment* ([. . . mènt]) and similar forms.

Now consider the word *condensation*. In an early cycle we assign main stress to the second syllable of *condense*. In the next cycle the rules apply to the form *condensation* as a whole, this being the next larger constituent. The suffix *-ion* always assigns main stress to the immediately preceding syllable, in this case, *ate*. Application of this rule weakens the syllable *dens* to secondary. The rule of vowel reduction does not apply to this vowel, since it is protected by secondary stress. Another rule of some generality replaces an initial stress sequence xxi by 231, and the rule of stress adjustment gives the final contour 3414. Thus the resulting form has a nonreduced vowel in the second syllable with stress four. Consider, in contrast, the word *compensation*. The second vowel of this word, also phonemically /e/ (cf. *compensatory*), has not received stress in any cycle before the word level at which the rule of vowel reduction applies (i.e. it is not derived from *compense* as *condensation* is derived from *condense*). It is therefore reduced to [ɨ]. We thus have a contrast of reduced and unreduced vowels with weak stress in *compensation-*

condensation as an automatic, though indirect, effect of difference in constituent structure.

As a final example, to illustrate the interweaving of Rules (15a) and (15b) as syntactic patterns grow more complex, consider the phrases *John's blackboard eraser, small boys' school* (meaning small school for boys), and *small boys school* (meaning school for small boys). These have the following derivations, after the initial cycles which assign main stress within the words:

I.1. [$_{NP}$ John's [$_N$[$_N$ black board]$_N$ eraser]$_N$]$_{NP}$

  2. [$_{NP}$ John's [$_N$ black board eraser]$_N$]$_{NP}$
(applying Rule (15a) to the innermost constituent and erasing brackets)

  3. [$_{NP}$ John's black board eraser]$_{NP}$
(applying Rule (15a) to the innermost constituent and erasing brackets)

  4. John's black board eraser
(applying Rule (15b) and erasing brackets)

II.1. [$_{NP}$ small [$_N$ boys' school]$_N$]$_{NP}$

  2. [$_{NP}$ small boys' school]$_{NP}$
(applying Rule (15a) to the innermost constituent and erasing brackets)

  3. small boys' school
(applying Rule (15b) and erasing brackets)

III.1. [$_N$[$_{NP}$ small boys]$_{NP}$ school]$_N$

  2. [$_N$ small boys school]$_N$
(applying Rule (15b) to the innermost constituent and erasing brackets)

  3. small boys school
(applying Rule (15a) and erasing brackets)

$$3 \quad 1 \quad 3$$
4. small boys school
   (by a rule of wide applicability that we have not given).

In short, a phonetic output that has an appearance of great complexity and disorder can be generated by systematic cyclic application of a small number of simple transformational rules, where the order of application is determined by what we know, on independent grounds, to be the syntactic structure of the utterance. It seems reasonable, therefore, to assume that rules of this kind underlie both the production and perception of actual speech. On this assumption we have a plausible explanation for the fact that native speakers uniformly and consistently produce and identify new sentences with these intricate physical characteristics (without, of course, any conscious awareness of the underlying processes or their phonetic effects). This suggests a somewhat novel theory of speech perception—that identifying an observed acoustic event as such-and-such a particular phonetic sequence is, in part, a matter of determining its syntactic structure (to this extent, understanding it). A more usual view is that we determine the phonetic and phonemic constitution of an utterance by detecting in the sound wave a sequence of physical properties, each of which is the defining property of some particular phoneme; we have already given some indication why this view (based on the linearity and invariance conditions for phonemic representation) is untenable.

'Formal analysis of natural languages', 306–18 in
Handbook of Mathematical Psychology, Vol. 11 (1963)

4.6 *The abstractness of phonological representations*

Knowledge of a language involves the ability to assign deep and surface structures to an infinite range of sentences, to relate these structures appropriately, and to assign a semantic interpretation and a phonetic interpretation to the paired deep and surface structures. This outline of the nature of grammar seems to be quite accurate as a first approximation of the characterization of 'knowledge of a language'. A person who knows a specific language has control of a grammar that *generates* (that is, characterizes) the infinite set of potential deep structures, maps them onto associated surface structures, and determines the semantic and phonetic interpretations of these abstract objects. From the information now available, it seems accurate to propose that the surface structure determines the phonetic interpretation completely and that the deep structure expresses those gram-

matical functions that play a role in determining the semantic interpretation, although certain aspects of the surface structure may also
participate in determining the meaning of the sentence in ways that I
will not discuss here. A grammar of this sort will therefore define a
certain infinite correlation of sound and meaning. It constitutes a
first step towards explaining how a person can understand an arbitrary
sentence of his language.

It is clear that the surface structure of a sentence is often misleading
and uninformative and that our knowledge of language involves
properties of a much more abstract nature, not indicated directly in
the surface structure. Furthermore, there is no possibility that we would
be able to account for linguistic competence in terms of 'habits',
'dispositions', 'knowing how', and other concepts associated with the
study of behaviour, as this study has been circumscribed, quite without
warrant, in recent years.

Even at the level of sound structure, there is evidence that abstract
representations are formed and manipulated in the mental operations
involved in language use. We have a more detailed understanding of
the nature of linguistic representation and the intricate conditions on
rule application in this domain than in any other. The work of the
past few years on sound structure seems to me to provide substantial
evidence in support of the view that the form of particular grammars
is determined, in highly significant ways, by a restrictive schematism
that specifies the choice of relevant phonetic properties, the kinds of
rules that can relate surface structure to phonetic representation, and
the conditions on organization and application of these rules. It thus
relates closely to the question of how this restrictive universal schematism comes to be used in language acquisition. Furthermore, these
investigations of sound structure, in so far as they support the conclusion
that abstract phonological structures are manipulated by tightly
organized and intricate systems of rules, are relevant to the very
interesting problem of developing empirically adequate models of
performance. They suggest that all current approaches to problems of
perception and organization of behaviour suffer from a failure to
attribute sufficient depth and complexity to the mental processes that
must be represented in any model that attempts to come to grips with
the empirical phenomena. Space does not permit a detailed development of these topics, either with respect to the matter of phonological
structure or with respect to its potential significance for cognitive
psychology. However, one simple illustrative example, which is quite

typical, may give some idea of the nature of the evidence that is available and the conclusions to which it points.

Recall that the syntactic rules of the language generate an infinite set of surface structures, each of which is a labelled bracketing of a string of minimal elements. For example, in (16) we may take the minimal elements to be the items *a, wise, man, is, honest*:

(16)

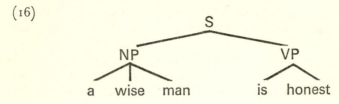

Each of these items can itself be represented as a string of segments, for example *man* as the string of segments /m/, /æ/, /n/. Each of these segments may be regarded in turn as a set of specified features; thus, /m/ stands for the feature complex [+consonantal], [−vocalic], [+nasal], and so on. The segmental constitution of an item will be given by a lexical entry—a characterization of the inherent phonetic semantic, and syntactic properties of the item in question. The lexicon of the language is the set of such lexical entries, with, perhaps, additional structure that need not concern us here. We are concerned now only with the phonetic properties of the lexical entry.

The lexical entry of an item must specify just those properties that are idiosyncratic, that are not determined by linguistic rule. For example, the lexical entry for *man* must indicate that its second segment is a low front vowel, but the degree of tenseness, diphthongization, nasalization, and so on, of this vowel need not be indicated in the lexical entry, since these are a matter of general rule, in part particular to various English dialects, in part common to all English dialects, in part a matter of universal phonology. Similarly, the lexical entry for *man* must indicate that it has an irregular plural, with the vowel shifting from low to mid. The segments of the lexical entry are abstract in the sense that the phonological rules of the language will frequently modify and elaborate them in a variety of ways; hence there need not be, in general, a simple point-by-point correspondence between the lexical entry and the actual phonetic representation. In discussing examples, I will use phonetic symbols in the usual way, each being regarded as a complex of a certain set of features. I will use the symbol

/   / to enclose lexical representations and the symbol [   ] to enclose all representations derived from lexical representations by application of phonological rules, including, in particular, the final phonetic representation derived by application of the full set of phonological rules.

Consider first such words as *sign-signify, paradigm-paradigmatic,* and so on. For reasons that will become clearer as we proceed, it is the derived form, in this case, that is most closely related to the underlying abstract lexical representation. Suppose, then, that we tentatively assign to the stem in these forms the lexical representations /sign/ and /pærædigm/, where the symbols have their conventional phonetic interpretation. Thus, the underlying element /sign/ is realized as phonetic [sign] before *-ify.* However, it is realized as phonetic [sayn] in isolation. A similar observation holds of *paradigm.*

The forms of *sign* and *paradigm* in isolation are determined by certain phonological rules that, operating jointly, have the effect of converting the representation /ig/ to [ay] when followed by a word-final nasal. A careful analysis of English phonology shows that this process can be broken into a sequence of steps, including the following (the second and third of which, in fact, require further analysis).

(17)   **a.** velar becomes continuant before word-final nasal
      b. vowel + velar continuant becomes tense vowel
      c. /ī/ becomes [ay] (where /ī/ is the tense segment corresponding to [i])

Applying these rules to underlying /sign/ in isolation, we derive first [siɣn] (where [ɣ] is the velar continuant) by (17a); then [sīn] by (17b); and finally [sayn] by (17c).

Rules (17a) and (17b) are of little interest, but (17c) is a part of a very general system of rules of 'vowel shift' that is quite central to English phonology. There are, for example, strong reasons for supposing that the stem underlying the forms *divine-divinity* is /divīn/, where the segment /ī/ is weakened to [i] before *-ity* and becomes [ay] by rule (17c) in isolation. Similarly, *reptile* derives from underlying /reptīl/, which becomes [reptayl] by (17c) in isolation and [reptil] before *-ian,* with the same shortening of vowel that takes place in *divinity;* and so on, in many other cases.

Consider next such words as *ignite-ignition, expedite-expeditious,* and *contrite-contrition.* Just as *reptile* and *divine* derive, by vowel shift, from /reptīl/ and /divīn/, so we can derive the first member of each of these pairs from /ignīt/, /expedīt/, and /contrīt/, respectively. The rule that applies to give the phonetic realization is (17c), a special case of the general process of vowel shift. Evidently, the second member of each pair is derived by such processes as (18) and (19):

(18) Vowels become nontense before *-ion*, *-ious*, *-ian*, *-ity*, and so on.

(19) The segment /t/ followed by a high front vowel is realized as [š].

The first of these rules is the one that gives [divin] from /divīn/ in *divinity* and [reptil] from /reptīl/ in *reptilian*. Similarly it gives [ignit] from /ignīt/ in *ignition*, [expedit] from /expedīt/ in *expeditious*, and [contrit] from /contrīt/ in *contrition*. There is an obvious underlying generalization, namely that a vowel becomes nontense before an unstressed vowel that is not in a word-final syllable; when properly formulated, this rule, along with vowel shift and a few others, constitutes the central portion of the English phonological system.

The second rule, (19), applies to the element /ti/ in /ignition/, /expeditious/, and /contrition/, replacing it by [š] and giving, finally, the phonetic realizations [igniš ən], [ekspədišəs], [kəntrišən], after the application of the rule that reduces unstressed vowels to [ə]. In short, the segments realized as [ayt] in *ignite*, *expedite*, and *contrite* are realized as [iš] in *ignition*, *expeditious*, and *contrition*.

But now consider the words *right-righteous*, phonetically [rayt]-[rayčəs]. The latter form appears to deviate from the regular pattern in two respects, namely in vowel quality (we would expect [i] rather than [ay], by rule (18)), and in the final consonant of the stem (we would expect [š] rather than [č], by rule (19)). If *right* were subject to the same processes as *expedite*, we would have [rišəs] rather than [rayčəs] as the phonetic realization, analogous to [ekspədišəs]. What is the explanation for this double deviation?

Notice first that rule (19) is not quite exact; there are, in fact, other cases in which /ti/ is realized as [č] rather than as [š], for example *question* [kwesčən], contrasted with *direction* [dərekšən]. A more accurate formulation would be (20):

(20) /t/ followed by a high front vowel is realized as [č] after a continuant and as [š] elsewhere.

Returning to the form *right*, we see that the final consonant would be correctly determined as [č] rather than [š] if in the underlying representation there were a continuant preceding it—that is, if the underlying representation were /riφt/, where φ is some continuant. The continuant φ must, furthermore, be distinct from any of the continuants that actually appear phonetically in this position, namely the dental, labial, or palatal continuants in the unitalicized portion of *wrist, rift,* or *wished.* We may assume, then, that φ is the velar continuant /x/, which does not, of course, appear phonetically in English. The underlying form, then, would be /rixt/.

Consider now the derivation of *right.* By rule (17b), the representation /rixt/ becomes [rīt]. By rule (17c), the representation /rīt/ becomes [rayt], which is the phonetic realization of *right.*

Consider next the derivation of *righteous.* Assuming that it has the same affix as *expeditious* and *repetitious,* we can represent it lexically as /rixtious/ (I do not concern myself here with the proper representation for *-ous*). Let us suppose that the ordering of the rules so far discussed is the following: (17a), (18), (20), (17b), (17c), an ordering consistent with other relevant facts of English, given certain simplifications for convenience of exposition. Rule (17a) is inapplicable and rule (18) is vacuous, when applied to the underlying form /rixtious/. Turning to rule (20), we see that it gives the form [rixčous]. Rule (17b) now applies, giving [rīčous], and rule (17c) gives [rayčous], which becomes [rayčǝs] by reduction of unstressed vowels. Thus by rules (20) and (17), which are independently motivated, the underlying representation /rixt/ will be realized phonetically as [rayt] in isolation and as [rayč] in *righteous,* exactly as required.

These facts strongly suggest that the underlying phonological representation must be /rixt/ (in accord with the orthography and, of course, the history). A sequence of rules that must be in the grammar for other reasons gives the alternation *right-righteous.* Therefore, this alternation is not at all exceptional, but rather perfectly regular. Of course, the underlying representation is quite abstract; it is connected with the superficial phonetic shape of the signal only by a sequence of interpretive rules.

Putting the matter differently, suppose that a person knows English but does not happen to have the vocabulary item *righteous.* Hearing this form for the first time, he must assimilate it to the system he has learned. If he were presented with the derived form [rišǝs], he would, of course, take the underlying representation to be exactly like that of *expedite, contrite,* and so on. But hearing [rayčǝs], he knows that this representation is impossible; although the consonantal distinction [š]-[č] might easily be missed under ordinary conditions of language use, the vocalic distinction [i]-[ay] would surely be obvious. Knowing the rules of English and hearing the vocalic element [ay] instead of [i], he knows that either the form is a unique exception or it contains a sequence /i/ followed by velar and is subject to rule (20). The velar must be a continuant, that is, /x/. But given that the velar is a continuant, it follows, if the form is regular (the null hypothesis, always), that the consonant must be [č], not [š], by rule (20). Thus, the hearer should perceive [rayčəs] rather than [rayšəs], even if the information as to the medial consonant is lacking in the received signal. Furthermore, the pressure to preserve regularity of alternations should act to block the superficial analogy to *expedite-expeditious* and *ignite-ignition*, and to preserve [č] as the phonetic realization of underlying /t/, as long as [ay] appears in place of expected [i], exactly as we observe to have occurred.

I do not mean this as a literal step-by-step account of how the form is learned, of course, but rather as a possible explanation of why the form resists a superficial (and in fact incorrect) analogy and preserves its status. We can explain the perception and preservation in the grammar of the [č]-[š] contrast in *righteous-expeditious* on the basis of the perceived distinction between [ay] and [i] and the knowledge of a certain system of rules. The explanation rests on the assumption that the underlying representations are quite abstract, and the evidence cited suggests that this assumption is, in fact, correct.

A single example can hardly carry much conviction. A careful investigation of sound structure, however, shows that there are a number of examples of this sort, and that, in general, highly abstract underlying structures are related to phonetic representations by a long sequence of rules, just as on the syntactic level abstract deep structures are in general related to surface structures by a long sequence of grammatical transformations. Assuming the existence of abstract mental representations and interpretive operations of this sort, we can find a surprising degree of organization underlying what appears superficially to be a chaotic arrangement of data, and in certain cases we can also explain why linguistic expressions are heard, used, and understood in certain ways. One cannot hope to determine either the underlying abstract forms or the processes that relate them to signals by introspection; there is, furthermore, no reason why one should find this consequence in any way surprising.

The explanation sketched above is at the level of particular rather than universal grammar, as this distinction was formulated earlier.

That is, we have accounted for a certain phenomenon on the basis of the assumption that certain rules appear in the internalized grammar, noting that these rules are, for the most part, independently motivated. Of course, considerations of universal grammar enter into this explanation in so far as they affect the choice of grammar on the basis of data. This interpenetration is unavoidable, as noted earlier. There are cases, however, where explicit principles of universal grammar enter more directly and clearly into a pattern of explanation. Thus, investigation of sound systems reveals certain very general principles of organization, some quite remarkable, governing phonological rules. For example, it has been observed that certain phonological rules operate in a cycle, in a manner determined by the surface structure. Recall that the surface structure can be represented as a labelled bracketing of the utterance, such as (16). In English, the very intricate phonological rules that determine stress contours and vowel reduction apply to phrases bounded by paired brackets in the surface structure, applying first to a minimal phrase of this sort, then to the next larger phrase, and so on, until the maximal domain of phonological processes is reached (in simple cases, the sentence itself). Thus, in the case of (16), the rules apply to the individual words (which, in a full description, would be assigned to categories and therefore bracketed), then to the phrases *a wise man* and *is honest*, and finally to the whole sentence. A few simple rules will give quite varied results, as the surface structures that determine their cyclic application vary.

Some simple effects of the principle of cyclic application are illustrated by such forms as those of (21):

(21)   **a.** *relaxation, emendation, elasticity, connectivity*
        b. *illustration, demonstration, devastation, anecdotal*

The unitalicized vowels are reduced to [ə] in (21b), but they retain their original quality in (21a). In some cases, we can determine the original quality of the reduced vowels of (21b) from other derived forms (for example, *illustrative, demonstrative*). The examples of (21a) differ from those of (21b) morphologically in that the former are derived from underlying forms (namely *relax, emend, elastic, connective*) that contain primary stress on the unitalicized vowel when these underlying forms appear in isolation; those of (21b) do not have this property. It is not difficult to show that vowel reduction in English, the replacement of a vowel by [ə], is contingent upon lack of stress. We can therefore account for the distinction between (21a) and (21b) by assuming the cyclic principle just formulated. In the case of (21a), on the first, innermost cycle, stress will be assigned by general rules to the unitalicized vowels. On the next cycle, stress is shifted*, but the abstract stress assigned on the first cycle is sufficient to protect the vowel from reduction. In the examples of (21b), earlier cycles never assign an abstract stress to the unitalicized vowel, which thus reduces. Observe that it is an *abstract* stress that protects the vowel from reduction. The actual, phonetic stress on the unitalicized nonreduced vowels is very weak; it would be stress 4, in the usual convention. In general, vowels with this weak a phonetic stress reduce, but in this case the abstract stress assigned in the earlier cycle prevents reduction. Thus, it is the abstract underlying representation that determines the phonetic form, a primary role being played by the abstract stress that is virtually eliminated in the phonetic form.

In this case, we can provide an explanation for a certain aspect of perception and articulation in terms of a very general abstract principle, namely the principle of cyclic application of rules stated on page 99. It is difficult to imagine how the language learner might derive this principle by 'induction' from the data presented to him. In fact, many of the effects of this principle relate to perception and have little or no analogue in the physical signal itself, under normal conditions of language use, so that the phenomena on which the induction would have to be based cannot be part of the experience of one who is not already making use of the principle. In fact, there is no procedure of induction or association that offers any hope of leading from such data as is available to a principle of this sort (unless, begging the question, we introduce the principle of cyclic application into the 'inductive procedure' in some manner). Therefore, the conclusion seems warranted that the principle of cyclic application of phonological rules is an innate organizing principle of universal grammar that is used in determining the character of linguistic experience and in constructing a grammar that constitutes the acquired knowledge of language. At the same time, this principle of universal grammar offers an explanation for such phenomena as were noted in (21).

Language and Mind (1968), 26–7, 32–8

---

* In 'connectivity', it is on the third cycle that the stress is shifted. The second cycle merely reassigns stress to the same syllable that is stressed on the first cycle. [C]

5 Syntax and Semantics

5.1 *Introductory*

[The problems that confront us when we try to define the place of 'semantics' (roughly, the theory of meaning) in a transformational generative theory of language are summed up by the following two questions. What are the precise differences, if any, between syntactic and semantic phenomena? Given that there are differences, what is the relationship between the syntactic and the semantic components of the grammar? The latter query resolves itself into a number of separate questions which are of the greatest importance for the development of linguistic theory. Thus, should the syntactic component act as input to the semantic component, that is, are syntactic phenomena not only independent of semantic phenomena but somehow 'prior' to them? Or should the reverse be the case, i.e. should the output of the semantic component act as input to the syntactic component? Further, if we decide that syntax should constitute the input to the semantic component, which syntactic subcomponent of the grammar should determine this input—the deep (or base) component, the surface (or transformational) component, or both? These questions are very much alive at the present time, and all the points of view suggested above (including the rejection of the difference between syntax and semantics) are represented in the current literature.

Traditionally, the difference between syntactic and semantic phenomena, or between 'grammar' and 'meaning', has been reflected by the difference between grammars and dictionaries, both of which have always been regarded as essential for the study of language. The need for a dictionary is demonstrated by the sentences in (1) which manifest certain meaning relations that apparently cannot be accounted for by grammar. The sentences are grammatically identical but differ in such a way that (i) and (ii) are interpreted as being different in meaning, while (ii) and (iii) are interpreted as having the same meaning.

(1) (i) The house is expensive.

    (ii) The car is expensive.

    (iii) The automobile is expensive.

There are other situations where no grammar hitherto conceived is able to account for all the relevant facts about sentences and their inter-relations. For example, some sentences are regarded as near-synonyms in spite of the fact that they have radically different syntactic structure (e.g. active-passive relationships), while other syntactically different sentences are not regarded as synonymous (e.g. positive-negative relationships).

The traditional division of linguistic data into grammatical and lexical phenomena captured the difference between semantic and syntactic representations but without stating the exact nature of the relationship between them. With the development of transformational generative theories of language it became clear that a linguistic description which treats the grammar and the lexicon as two separate entities without rules to inter-relate them cannot serve as a descriptively adequate specification of the facts of language, or of the competence of native speakers. Let us illustrate this point with an example from language learning. Any teacher of a foreign language knows that a student who is not a fluent speaker is unable to construct 'correct' sentences in the target language on the basis of information in the grammar and the dictionary alone. In addition to this information he needs to take account of the semantic relations between words in a sentence. If a non-fluent speaker is not provided with rules for the selection of those words which are appropriate in a given sentence context, he is liable to construct grammatically correct* sentences which 'make no sense', or which contain words 'used in the wrong sense' given a particular syntactic environment. On the other hand, a fluent speaker has the ability to distinguish semantically anomalous sentences from semantically regular ones. He can also detect semantic ambiguities ('The bank is green' may refer to a building or to a river bank), and he knows when two sentences with different syntactic structures are paraphrases of each other.

In view of these facts, linguistics has recently become concerned with the relations between syntax and semantics, and the possibility of achieving some degree of integration between these two areas of

---

* Note that this presupposes a distinction between 'grammatically correct' and 'semantically correct'. [A, B]

linguistic description. Chomsky's approach to the semantic interpretation of sentences is based on the work of Katz and Fodor, which was incorporated into Katz and Postal's *Integrated theory of linguistic descriptions* (1964). Recently, however, Chomsky has departed from these proposals in one important respect. The nature of this modification to the theory will be discussed below.

Katz and Fodor (1963) define the semantic component of a linguistic theory as a 'projection device' which interprets abstract syntactic objects and which consists of a dictionary and a set of projection rules. An ideal dictionary will provide a meaning for each of the lexical items in the language, and the projection rules will assign a semantic interpretation to the strings which are generated by the syntactic base component. Note that in this system semantic interpretations are assigned uniquely to deep structures rather than to surface structures. The reason for this is suggested by the sentence 'visiting aunts can be boring' where in order to assign an unambiguous semantic interpretation to the sentence we need access to information contained in its deep structure.

According to Katz and Fodor, each lexical item in the deep string 'receives a meaning' on the basis of semantic information provided in the dictionary. The projection rules then combine the meanings of the individual lexical items to arrive at a meaning for the whole sentence. This arrangement is the formal expression of a speaker's ability to understand any new sentence on the basis of the words which it contains, and which the speaker already knows. However, a speaker does not obtain a meaning for a sentence on the basis of lexical items alone. He is able to determine meanings not only for individual words and whole sentences, but also for the significant sub-parts of sentences, such as Noun Phrase, Verb Phrase, etc. The projection rules reconstruct these aspects of a speaker's semantic competence by 'working upwards' through the various levels of constituent structure, establishing a reading for each constituent of the sentence before they yield a reading for the sentence as a whole.

It is evident that these proposals reflect Chomsky's insistence on the independence of syntax (see p. 18). According to this view of the interrelation between syntax and semantics, the grammar must be organized in such a way that the output of the syntactic base component constitutes the input to the semantic component. In other words, the base component in its capacity of defining deep syntactic structures occupies the central place in Chomsky's theory of language.

Katz and Postal's requirement that semantic interpretations are assigned uniquely to deep structures means that the transformational sub-component of the syntactic component does not contribute in any way to semantic interpretation. Hence the dictum 'transformations don't change meaning'. As we saw in Chapter 3, this arrangement of the grammar constituted a significant departure from Chomsky's proposals in *Syntactic Structures* where the input to the transformational component consisted of a set of simple kernel strings and, for example, a kernel string could be made negative or imperative by means of the relevant transformations. It followed automatically from this arrangement that the transformations must have important semantic consequences. However, according to Katz and Postal's subsequent proposals (1964) the fact whether a sentence is negative or imperative is indicated in the base component by the use of an optional 'marker' NEG or IMP. These 'markers' are interpreted directly by the semantic component so that the operation of the negative transformation is merely conditional on choosing the symbol NEG. In other words the negative transformation is semantically vacuous and merely specifies the syntactic consequences of choosing the symbol NEG (e.g. where to locate the element *not* in the sentence). Chomsky has recently argued that this restriction on the nature of transformations is too strong and that there are cases where transformations have semantic effects, although these may be of a limited nature.

For example, one of the properties of the present perfect aspect in English is that it carries the presupposition that the subject is alive. Thus, knowing that Einstein is dead, we would not say 'Einstein has taught me physics' but rather 'Einstein taught me physics'. But now consider what happens if we use the passive form with present perfect aspect. In this case it is possible to say 'I have been taught physics by Einstein', since the passive form does not carry the presupposition that Einstein is alive. It seems, then, that active and passive forms in English may differ in the presuppositions they express. In the examples quoted the surface structure contributes to the meaning of the sentence, and it follows that the passive transformation must have semantic effects.

Another example is provided by the interrogative transformation when it applies to sentences containing a modal as the auxiliary constituent. It is clear that the sentences 'I shall open the window' and 'Shall I open the window?' are quite different in meaning over and above the fact that the one is declarative and the other interrogative.

The second sentence is not merely a request for an answer, it is also an implicit request for advice or a decision. Consequently, it seems that in this case the interrogative transformation has semantic implications and is not merely 'triggered off' by a 'marker' Q in the base component.

Considerations of this nature lead us to the view that the semantic component does not operate solely on the output of the deep syntactic component but also on the output of the transformational component. This, in brief, constitutes Chomsky's recent departure from the standard theory set out in Katz and Postal (1964) and Chomsky (1965). The difference between the standard theory and the modified theory concerning input-output relations may be represented diagrammatically as follows:

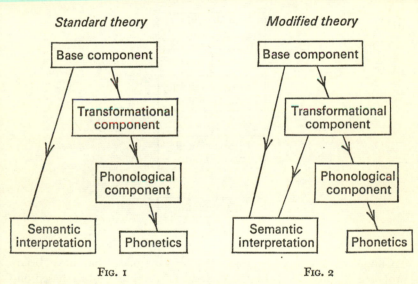

FIG. 1   FIG. 2

Some linguists have argued that the meaning differences between active and passive, and between modal-interrogative and modal-declarative referred to above could all be expressed in the deep component of the grammar, if the deep component were of a semantic rather than of a syntactic nature or, more significantly, if the difference between the semantic component and the deep syntactic component were obliterated. If this suggestion were to be adopted the semantic component would cease to be an interpretative projection-device of the type described by Katz and Postal and would instead define a (presumably) infinite set of semantic representations which would serve as a direct input to the syntactic transformational component. Hence the expression 'semantically-based grammar' or 'semantic grammars'. It would also be a consequence of these proposals that the independent deep syntactic component of the standard theory would cease to exist as an independent level of description.

The basically unilinear structure of the input-output relations of a semantically-based grammar, as opposed to the triangular organization of the standard theory (see Figs. 1 and 2, p. 105) may be represented diagrammatically as follows:

Semantic grammars

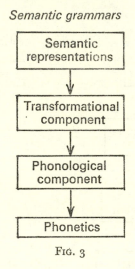

FIG. 3

Chomsky's objections to the semantic grammars that have been proposed (notably by J. McCawley and C. F. Fillmore) are based on three arguments. Either semantic grammars do not tally with the facts of language, or they are logically inconsistent, or they are mere notational variants of the standard theory, i.e. they are the same in substance but different in expression.

In 5.2 Chomsky denies that there is a procedure for determining the semantic features of an utterance independently of the grammar, and further procedures for determining the syntax (or phonology) of the language from these independently motivated semantic properties. Nevertheless, syntactic categories and processes will relate, in some way, to meaning and language use, just as phonological categories and processes relate, in some way, to physical and perceptual reality. The establishment of an independent deep syntax does not rule out the possibility that there may be some semantic considerations which are relevant in grammar. Whether or not this is the case remains an open question at the present time.

The first of the following extracts is from *Syntactic Structures* (1957). The other extracts are from *Aspects of the Theory of Syntax* (1965). In *Syntactic Structures* Chomsky is concerned with problems of syntactic rather than semantic description, and semantics tends to be considered from the point of view of the *use* of language. The emphasis changes in *Aspects*, where one of Chomsky's main concerns is the interrelation between syntax and semantics in a competence model of grammar. [A, B]]

5.2 *Formal and semantic features in language*

In proposing that syntactic structure can provide a certain insight into problems of meaning and understanding we have entered onto dangerous ground. There is no aspect of linguistic study more subject to confusion and more in need of clear and careful formulation than that which deals with the points of connection between syntax and semantics. The real question that should be asked is: 'How are the syntactic devices available in a given language put to work in the actual use of this language?' Instead of being concerned with this very important problem, however, the study of interconnections between syntax and semantics has largely been dominated by a side issue and a misformulated question. The issue has been whether or not semantic information is required for discovering or selecting a grammar; and the challenge usually posed by those who take the affirmative in this dispute is: 'How can you construct a grammar with no appeal to meaning?'

The question itself, however, is wrongly put, since the implication that obviously one can construct a grammar *with* appeal to meaning is totally unsupported. One might with equal justification ask: 'How can you construct a grammar with no knowledge of the hair colour of speakers?' The question that should be raised is: 'How can you construct a grammar?' I am not acquainted with any detailed attempt to develop the theory of grammatical structure in partially semantic terms or any specific and rigorous proposal for the use of semantic information in constructing or evaluating grammars. It is undeniable that 'intuition about linguistic form' is very useful to the investigator of linguistic form (i.e. grammar). It is also quite clear that the major goal of grammatical theory is to replace this obscure reliance on intuition by some rigorous and objective approach. There is, however, little evidence that 'intuition about meaning' is at all useful in the actual investigation of linguistic form. I believe that the inadequacy of suggestions about the use of meaning in grammatical analysis fails to be apparent only because of their vagueness and because of an unfortunate tendency to confuse 'intuition about linguistic form' with 'intuition about meaning', two terms that have in common only their vagueness and their undesirability in linguistic theory. However, because of the widespread acceptance of such suggestions, it may be worth while to investigate some of them briefly, even though the burden of proof in this case rests completely on the linguist who claims to have been able to develop some grammatical notion in semantic terms.

Among the more common assertions put forth as supporting the dependence of grammar on meaning we have the following:

(3)   (i)   two utterances are phonemically distinct if and only if they differ in meaning;

    (ii)   morphemes are the smallest elements that have meaning;

    (iii)   grammatical sentences are those that have semantic significance;

    (iv)   the grammatical relation subject-verb (i.e. *NP–VP* as an analysis of *Sentence*) corresponds to the general 'structural meaning' actor-action;

    (v)   the grammatical relation verb-object (i.e. *Verb–NP* as an analysis of *VP*) corresponds to the structural meaning action-goal or action-object of action;

    (vi)   an active sentence and the corresponding passive are synonymous.

A great many linguists have expressed the opinion that phonemic distinctness must be defined in terms of differential meaning (synonymity, to use a more familiar term), as proposed in (3). However, it is immediately evident that (3i) cannot be accepted, as it stands, as a definition of phonemic distinctness. If we are not to beg the question, the utterances in question must be tokens, not types. But there are utterance tokens that are phonemically distinct and identical in meaning (synonyms) and there are utterance tokens that are phonemically identical and different in meaning (homonyms). Hence (3i) is false in both directions. From left to right it is falsified by such pairs as 'bachelor' and 'unmarried man', or, even more seriously, by such absolute synonyms as /ekĭnámiks/ and /iykĭnámiks/ ('economics'), 'ádult' and 'adúlt', /rǽšĭn/ and réyšĭn/, ('ration'), and many others, which may coexist even within one style of speech. From right to left, (3i) is falsified by such pairs as 'bank' (of a river) and 'bank' (for savings)*, 'metal' and 'medal' (in many dialects), and numerous other examples. In other words, if we assign two utterance tokens to the same utterance type on the basis of (3i), we will simply get the wrong classification in a large number of cases.

It is, of course, impossible to prove that semantic notions are of no use in grammar, just as it is impossible to prove the irrelevance of any other given set of notions. Investigation of such proposals, however, invariably seems to lead to the conclusion that only a purely formal basis can provide a firm and productive foundation for the construction of grammatical theory. Detailed investigation of each semantically oriented proposal would go beyond the bounds of this study, and would be rather pointless, but we can mention briefly some of the more obvious counter-examples to such familiar suggestions as (3).

Such morphemes as 'to' in 'I want to go' or the dummy carrier 'do' in 'did he come?' can hardly be said to have a meaning in any independent sense, and it seems reasonable to assume that an independent notion of meaning, if clearly given, may assign meaning of some sort to such non-morphemes as *gl-* in 'gleam', 'glimmer', 'glow'. Thus we have counter-examples to the suggestion (3ii) that morphemes be defined as minimal meaning-bearing elements. In section 1.3 we have given grounds for rejecting 'semantic significance' as a general criterion for grammaticalness, as proposed in (3iii). Such sentences as 'John received a letter' or 'the fighting stopped' show clearly the untenability of the assertion (3iv) that the grammatical relation subject-verb has the 'structural meaning' actor-action, if meaning is taken seriously as a concept independent of grammar. Similarly, the assignment (3v) of any such structural meaning as action-goal to the verb-object relation as such is precluded by such sentences as 'I will disregard his

* Note that we cannot argue that 'bank' in 'the river bank' and 'bank' in 'the savings bank' are two occurrences of the same word, since this is precisely the question under investigation. To say that two utterance tokens are occurrences of the same word is to say that they are not phonemically distinct, and presumably this is what the synonymity criterion (3i) is supposed to determine for us. [C]

incompetence' or 'I missed the train'. In contradiction to (3vi), we can describe circumstances in which a 'quantificational' sentence such as 'everyone in the room knows at least two languages' may be true, while the corresponding passive 'at least two languages are known by everyone in the room' is false, under the normal interpretation of these sentences—e.g. if one person in the room knows only French and German, and another only Spanish and Italian. This indicates that not even the weakest semantic relation (factual equivalence) holds in general between active and passive.

These counter-examples should not, however, blind us to the fact that there are striking correspondences between the structures and elements that are discovered in formal, grammatical analysis and specific semantic functions. None of the assertions of (3) is wholly false; some are very nearly true. It seems clear, then, that undeniable, though only imperfect correspondences hold between formal and semantic features in language. The fact that the correspondences are so inexact suggests that meaning will be relatively useless as a basis for grammatical description. Careful analysis of each proposal for reliance on meaning confirms this, and shows, in fact, that important insights and generalizations about linguistic structure may be missed if vague semantic clues are followed too closely. For example, we have seen that the active-passive relation is just one instance of a very general and fundamental aspect of formal linguistic structure. The similarity between active-passive, negation, declarative-interrogative, and other transformational relations would not have come to light if the active-passive relation had been investigated exclusively in terms of such notions as synonymity.

The fact that correspondences between formal and semantic features exist, however, cannot be ignored. These correspondences should be studied in some more general theory of language that will include a theory of linguistic form and a theory of the use of language as subparts. Having determined the syntactic structure of the language, we can study the way in which this syntactic structure is put to use in the actual functioning of language. An investigation of the semantic function of level structure might be a reasonable step towards a theory of the interconnections between syntax and semantics. In fact, the correlations between the form and use of language can even provide certain rough criteria of adequacy for a linguistic theory and the grammars to which it leads. We can judge formal theories in terms of their ability to explain and clarify a variety of facts about the way in which sentences are used and understood. In other words, we should like the syntactic framework of the language that is isolated and exhibited by the grammar to be able to support semantic description, and we shall naturally rate more highly a theory of formal structure that leads to grammars that meet this requirement more fully.

Phrase structure and transformational structure appear to provide the major syntactic devices available in language for organization and expression of content. The grammar of a given language must show how these abstract structures are actually realized in the case of the language in question, while linguistic theory must seek to clarify these foundations for grammar and the methods for evaluating and choosing between proposed grammars.

It is important to recognize that by attempting to deal with grammar and semantics and their points of connection, we need not alter the purely formal character of the theory of grammatical structure itself. In the earlier sections of this book we have outlined the development of some fundamental linguistic concepts in purely formal terms. We considered the problem of syntactic research to be that of constructing a device for producing a given set of grammatical sentences and of studying the properties of grammars that do this effectively. Such semantic notions as reference, significance, and synonymity played no role in the discussion. The outlined theory, of course, had serious gaps in it—in particular, the assumption that the set of grammatical sentences is given in advance is clearly too strong, and the notion of 'simplicity' to which appeal was made explicitly or tacitly was left unanalysed. However, neither these nor other gaps in this development of grammatical theory can be filled in or narrowed, to my knowledge, by constructing this theory on a partially semantic basis.

So far, then, we have been studying language as an instrument or a tool, attempting to describe its structure with no explicit reference to the way in which this instrument is put to use. The motivation for this self-imposed formality requirement for grammars is quite simple—there seems to be no other basis that will yield a rigorous, effective, and 'revealing' theory of linguistic structure. The requirement that this theory shall be a completely formal discipline is perfectly compatible with the desire to formulate it in such a way as to have suggestive and significant interconnections with a parallel semantic theory. In fact, this formal study of the structure of language as an instrument may be expected to provide insight into the actual use of language, i.e. into the process of understanding sentences.

To understand a sentence we must know much more than the analysis of this sentence on each linguistic level. We must also know the reference and meaning of the morphemes or words of which it is composed; naturally, grammar cannot be expected to be of much help here. These notions form the subject matter for semantics. In describing the meaning of a word it is often expedient, or necessary, to refer to the syntactic framework in which this word is usually embedded; e.g. in describing the meaning of 'hit' we would no doubt describe the agent and object of the action in terms of the notions 'subject' and 'object', which are apparently best analysed as purely formal notions belonging to the theory of grammar. We shall naturally find that a great many words or morphemes of a single grammatical category are described semantically in partially similar terms, e.g. verbs in terms of subject and object, etc. This is not surprising; it means that the syntactic devices available in the language are being used fairly systematically. We have seen, however, that to generalize from this fairly systematic use and to assign 'structural meanings' to grammatical categories or constructions just as 'lexical meanings' are assigned to words or morphemes, is a step of very questionable validity.

Another common but dubious use of the notion 'structural meaning' is with reference to the meanings of so-called 'grammatically functioning' morphemes such as *ing*, *ly*, prepositions, etc. The contention that the meanings of these morphemes are fundamentally different from the meanings of nouns, verbs, adjectives, and perhaps other large classes, is often supported by appeal to the fact that these morphemes can be distributed in a sequence of blanks or nonsense syllables so as to give the whole the appearance of a sentence, and in fact, so as to determine the grammatical category of the nonsense elements. For example, in the sequence 'Pirots karulize elatically' we know that the three words are noun, verb and adverb by virtue of the *s*, *ize*, and *ly* respectively. But this property does not sharply distinguish 'grammatical' morphemes from others, since in such sequences as 'the Pirots karul — yesterday' or 'give him — water' the blanks are also determined as a variant of past tense, in the first case, and as 'the', 'some', etc., but not 'a', in the second. The fact that in these cases we were forced to give blanks rather than nonsense words is explained by the productivity or 'open-endedness' of the categories Noun, Verb, Adjective, etc., as opposed to the categories Article, Verbal Affix, etc. In general, when we distribute a sequence of morphemes in a sequence of blanks we limit the choice of elements that can be placed in the unfilled positions to form a grammatical sentence. Whatever differences there are among morphemes with respect to this property are apparently better explained in terms of such grammatical notions as productivity, freedom of combination, and size of substitution class than in terms of any presumed feature of meaning.

Syntactic Structures, 93–5, 100–5

5.3 *The boundaries of syntax and semantics*

[At this point the problem of the relationship between syntax and semantics is taken up again in the context of *Aspects of the Theory of Syntax* (1965). It will be recalled that in section 3.2 (p. 43) we examined the sentence 'sincerity may frighten the boy' and found that, concerning this sentence, a traditional grammar might provide three types of information. Two types of information, i.e. categorial and functional, were discussed in section 3.2. We now turn to the third type of information, which is repeated in (4):

(4)   The N *boy* is a Count Noun (as distinct from the Mass Noun *butter* and the Abstract Noun *sincerity*) and a Common Noun (as distinct from the Proper Noun *John* and the Pronoun *it*); it is, furthermore, an Animate Noun (as distinct from *book*) and a Human Noun (as distinct from *bee*); *frighten* is a Transitive Verb (as distinct from *occur*), and one that does not freely permit Object deletion (as distinct from *read, eat*); it takes Progressive Aspect freely (as distinct from *know, own*); it allows Abstract Subjects (as distinct from *eat, admire*) and Human Objects (as distinct from *read, wear*).]

Information of the sort presented in (4) raises several difficult and rather vexing questions. First, it is not obvious to what extent this information should be provided by the syntactic component at all. Second, it is an interesting question whether or to what extent semantic considerations are relevant in determining such subcategorizations as those involved in (4). These are distinct questions, though they are often confused. They are connected only in that if the basis for making the distinctions is purely syntactic, then surely the information must be presented in the syntactic component of the grammar. We might call these the questions of *presentation* and *justification*, respectively.

As far as the question of justification is concerned, a linguist with a serious interest in semantics will presumably attempt to deepen and extend syntactic analysis to the point where it can provide the information concerning subcategorization, instead of relegating this to un-analysed semantic intuition, there being, for the moment, no other available proposal as to a semantic basis for making the necessary distinctions. Of course, it is an open question whether this attempt can succeed, even in part.

I shall be concerned here only with the question of *presentation* of information of the sort given in (4). I am assuming throughout that the semantic component of a generative grammar, like the phonological component, is purely interpretive. It follows that all information utilized in semantic interpretation must be presented in the syntactic component of the grammar (but cf. p. 120). Some of the problems involved in presenting this information will be explored later.

Although the question of justification of subcategorizations such as those of (4) is beyond the scope of the present discussion, it may nevertheless be useful to touch on it briefly. What is at stake, essentially, is the status of such expressions as

(5)   (i)   the boy may frighten sincerity
      (ii) sincerity may admire the boy
      (iii) John amazed the injustice of that decision
      (iv) the boy elapsed
      (v)   the boy was abundant
      (vi) the harvest was clever to agree
      (vii) John is owning a house
     (viii) the dog looks barking
      (ix) John solved the pipe
      (x)   the book dispersed

It is obvious to anyone who knows English that these expressions have an entirely different status from such sentences as

(6)   (i)   sincerity may frighten the boy
       (ii) the boy may admire sincerity
       (iii) the injustice of that decision amazed John
       (iv) a week elapsed
       (v)   the harvest was abundant
       (vi) the boy was clever to agree
       (vii) John owns a house
      (viii) the dog looks terrifying
       (ix) John solved the problem
       (x)   the boys dispersed

The distinction between (5) and (6) is not at issue, and clearly must be

accounted for somehow by an adequate theory of sentence interpreta
tion (a descriptively adequate grammar). The expressions of (5)
deviate in some manner (not necessarily all in the same manner)
from the rules of English. If interpretable at all, they are surely not
interpretable in the manner of the corresponding sentences of (6).
Rather, it seems that interpretations are imposed on them by virtue of
analogies that they bear to nondeviant sentences.

There are fairly clear-cut cases of violation of purely syntactic
rules, for example,

(7)   (i)   sincerity frighten may boy the
      (ii)   boy the frighten may sincerity

and standard examples of purely semantic (or 'pragmatic') incongruity, for example,

(8)   (i)   oculists are generally better trained than eye-doctors
      (ii)   both of John's parents are married to aunts of mine
      (iii) I'm memorizing the score of the sonata I hope to compose
             some day
      (iv)   that ice cube that you finally managed to melt just shattered
      (v)   I knew you would come, but I was wrong

The examples of (5), however have a borderline character, and it is
much less clear how their aberrant status is to be explained. In other
words, we must face the problem of determining to what extent the
results and methods of syntactic or of semantic analysis can be extended
to account for the deviance and interpretation of these expressions.
It goes without saying that the same answer may not be appropriate
in all of these cases, and that purely semantic or purely syntactic
considerations may not provide the answer in some particular case.
In fact, it should not be taken for granted, necessarily, that syntactic
and semantic considerations can be sharply distinguished.

5.4 *Degrees of grammaticalness*

The distinction between strict subcategorization features and selectional features, which is formally well defined (cf. p. 55) appears to
correlate rather closely with an important distinction in language use.
Each such contextual feature is associated with a certain rule that
limits lexical entries containing this feature to certain contexts. We can,
in each case, construct a deviant sentence by breaking the rule. Thus
in section 3, Verbs are strictly subcategorized into Intransitives,

Transitives, pre-Adjectival, pre-Sentence, etc. In these cases, violation of the rules will give such strings as:

(9)   (i) John found sad
       (ii) John elapsed that Bill will come
       (iii) John compelled
       (iv) John became Bill to leave
       (v) John persuaded great authority to Bill

On the other hand, failure to observe a selectional rule will give such typical examples as

(10)   (i) colourless green ideas sleep furiously
        (ii) golf plays John
        (iii) the boy may frighten sincerity
        (iv) misery loves company
        (v) they perform their leisure with diligence

Clearly, strings such as (9) that break strict subcategorization rules and strings such as (10) that break selectional rules are deviant. It is necessary to impose an interpretation on them somehow—this being a task that varies in difficulty or challenge from case to case—whereas there is no question of imposing an interpretation in the case of such strictly well-formed sentences as

(11)   (i) revolutionary new ideas appear infrequently
        (ii) John plays golf
        (iii) sincerity may frighten the boy
        (iv) John loves company
        (v) they perform their duty with diligence

Nevertheless, the manner of deviation illustrated in (10) is rather different from that in (9). Sentences that break selectional rules can often be interpreted metaphorically (particularly, as personification—cf. Bloomfield, 1963) or allusively in one way or another, if an appropriate context of greater or less complexity is supplied. That is, these sentences are apparently interpreted by a direct analogy to well-formed sentences that observe the selectional rules in question. Clearly, one would proceed in quite a different way if forced to assign an interpretation to sentences that break strict subcategorization rules, for example, the sentences of (9).

These examples are, I think, typical of a fairly wide class of cases. A descriptively adequate grammar should make all of these distinctions on some formal grounds, and a grammar of the type just described seems to make them in some measure, at least. It distinguishes perfectly well-formed sentences such as (11) from the sentences of (9) and (10), which are not directly generated by the system of grammatical rules. It further separates the sentences of (9), generated by relaxing strict subcategorization rules, from sentences such as (10), which are generated when selectional rules are relaxed. Thus it takes several steps toward the development of a significant theory of 'degree of grammaticalness'*.

It seems that sentences deviating from selectional rules that involve 'higher-level' lexical features such as [Count] are much less acceptable and are more difficult to interpret than those that involve such 'lower-level' features as [Human]. At the same time, it is important to bear in mind that not all rules involving low-level syntactic features tolerate deviation as readily as do selectional rules involving these features. Thus both of the sentences

(12) (i) the book who you read was a best seller
      (ii) who you met is John

result from failure to observe rules involving the feature [Human], but are totally unacceptable—although of course an interpretation can easily, and no doubt uniformly, be imposed on them. Both in degree of acceptability and manner of interpretation, they differ completely from sentences that result from a failure to observe selectional rules involving the feature [Human]. Thus no matter how selectional rules are treated, there is no doubt that such features as [Human] play a role in purely syntactic rules (since surely the examples of (12) are ruled out on purely syntactic grounds).

* To avoid what has been a persistent misunderstanding, it must be emphasized that 'grammaticalness' is being used here as a technical term, with no implication that deviant sentences are being 'legislated against' as 'without a function' or 'illegitimate'. Quite the contrary is true, as has repeatedly been stressed and illustrated in discussions of generative grammar. The question as to whether the grammar should generate deviant sentences is purely terminological, having to do with nothing more than the technical sense of 'generate'. A descriptively adequate grammar must assign to each string a structural description that indicates the manner of its deviation from strict well-formedness (if any). A natural terminological decision would be to say that the grammar *directly generates the language* consisting of just the sentences that do not deviate at all (such as (11)), with their structural descriptions. The grammar *derivatively generates* all other strings (such as (9) and (10)), with their structural descriptions. These structural descriptions will indicate the manner and degree of deviance of the derivatively generated sentences. [C]

Similarly, consider the selectional feature [[+Abstract] ... — ... [+Animate]] assigned to such Verbs as *frighten, amuse, charm,* ... This feature is involved in rules that are as inviolable as those that give *the book which you read was a best seller* and *what you found was my book,* while excluding (12). Thus items that are positively specified with respect to this feature can appear in the position of pure Adjectives, so that we have such sentences as *a very frightening (amusing, charming, ...) person suddenly appeared,* but not, for example,

(13) (i) a very walking person appeared
      (ii) a very hitting person appeared

These sentences, like those of (12), are immediately and perhaps uniquely interpretable, but are obviously much more seriously ungrammatical, in the intuitive sense that we are now attempting to explicate, than the examples of violation of selectional rules given earlier. Thus it seems that this selectionally introduced contextual feature is also involved in rules that cannot be violated without serious departure from grammaticalness.

Examples such as (12) and (13) therefore support two important observations. First, it is clear that features such as [Human] and [[+Abstract] ... — ... [+Animate]] play a role in the functioning of the syntactic component, no matter how narrowly syntax is conceived, as long as it is agreed that (12) and (13) are syntactically deviant. The special character of the examples of (10) is not attributable to the fact that these sentences violate rules involving 'low-level features', but rather to the fact that the rules that they violate are selectional rules. Second, it is clear from such examples as (12) and (13) that the notion 'grammaticalness' cannot be related to 'interpretability' (ease, uniqueness, or uniformity of interpretation), in any simple way, at least. There are sentences such as (12) and (13) that are uniquely, uniformly, and immediately interpretable, no doubt, although they are paradigm examples of departure from well-formedness. On the other hand, there are also perfectly well-formed sentences that may pose great difficulties for interpretation, and may be subject to a variety of perhaps conflicting interpretations. More generally, it is clear that the intuitive notion of grammatical well-formedness is by no means a simple one and that an adequate explication of it will involve theoretical constructs of a highly abstract nature, just as it is clear that various diverse factors determine how and whether a sentence can be interpreted.

The attempts of some linguists to give a precise definition to at least one dimension of degree of grammaticalness are much more plausible if limited to the question of deviation from selectional rules than if extended to the full range of examples of deviation from well-formedness. In fact, following this suggestion, we might conclude that the *only* function of the selectional rules is to impose a hierarchy of deviation from grammaticalness on a certain set of sentences, namely those sentences that can be generated by selectional constraints while otherwise keeping the grammar unchanged.

Observe that the rules of the grammar impose a partial ordering in terms of dominance among the features that constitute a complex symbol in a Phrase-marker.

Let us suppose that the formative *frighten* is accompanied by a complex symbol consisting of the features [+V,+—NP,+[+Abstract] ...—... [+Animate]], and others, and that the rules of the grammar impose the dominance order [+V], [+—NP], [+[+Abstract] ... — ... [+Animate]]. (For an interpretation of these features see section 3.3, p. 46.)

In terms of this order, we can define the *degree of deviation* of a string that results from substituting a lexical item in the position of *frighten* in this Phrase-marker. The deviation is greater the higher in the dominance hierarchy is the feature corresponding to the rule that is relaxed. In the example given, then, deviance would be greatest if the item substituted for *frighten* is a non-Verb, less great if it is a Verb but a non-Transitive Verb, and still less great if it is a Transitive Verb that does not take an Abstract Subject. Thus we should have the following order of deviance:

(14)   (i) sincerity may virtue the boy
      (ii) sincerity may elapse the boy
     (iii) sincerity may admire the boy

This seems to give a natural explication for at least one sense of the term 'deviance'. Elsewhere, it has been suggested that size of category within which substitution takes place may determine the degree of grammaticalness (the extent of syntactic deviance) of a string.

It appears that features introduced by strict subcategorization rules dominate features introduced by selectional rules; and that all lexical features are dominated by the symbols for lexical categories. Furthermore, deviation from selectional rules involving high-level features is apparently more serious than deviation from selectional rules involving

9

lower-level features. These various observations combine to make the definition of 'degree of deviance' just proposed a rather natural one. If the distinction between strict subcategorization rules and selectional rules noted earlier is generally valid, we might go on to superimpose on the scale of deviance a split into perhaps three general types, namely the types that result from: (i) violation of lexical category (such as (14i)); (ii) conflict with a strict subcategorization feature (such as (14ii) and (9)); and (iii) conflict with a selectional feature (such as (14iii) and (10)). There are, furthermore, subdivisions within at least the third type. Of course, there are also many other types (such as (12), (13))*. This is not surprising, since there are rules of many kinds that can be violated.

5.5 *The role of selectional rules*

Selectional rules play a rather marginal role in the grammar, although the features that they deal with may be involved in many purely syntactic processes (cf. (12), (13)). One might propose therefore, that selectional rules be dropped from the syntax and that their function be taken over by the semantic component. Such a change would do little violence to the structure of grammar as described earlier. Of course, the features that are utilized and introduced by selectional rules would still appear in lexical entries for strings. That is, *boy* would be specified as [+Human] and *frighten* as permitting an Abstract Subject and Animate Object, etc., in the lexical entries for these items. Furthermore, if we continue to call a feature of the lexical entry a 'syntactic feature' when it is involved in a strictly syntactic rule, then these features of the lexical entry will be syntactic rather than semantic features (cf. the discussion of (12), (13)). Nevertheless, in accordance with this proposal, the grammar will directly generate even such sentences as (10), though not, of course, (9), as syntactically well

---

* These examples do not begin to exhaust the range of possibilities that must be considered in a full study of interpretation of deviant sentences. For one thing, they do not illustrate the use of order-inversion as a stylistic device. The discussion of deviation from grammaticalness that has been carried on here offers no insight into this phenomenon. For example, consider the following line: 'Me up at does/out of the floor/quietly Stare/a poisoned mouse/still who alive/is asking What/have i done that/You wouldn't have' (E. E. Cummings). This poses not the slightest difficulty or ambiguity of interpretation, and it would surely be quite beside the point to try to assign it a degree of deviation in terms of the number or kind of rules of the grammar that are violated in generating it. [C]

formed. The syntactic component of the grammar would not, in other words, impose a hierarchy of degree of grammaticalness at these lower levels of deviation. This task would now have to be taken over by the semantic component.

Consider such a typical case of violation of selectional rules as:

(15)   John frightened sincerity

This is a deviant sentence, formed by relaxing the restriction of *frighten* to Animate Direct-Objects. Nevertheless, there are frames in which this restriction can be violated with no consequent unnaturalness, as, for example, in

(16)   (i) it is nonsense to speak of (there is no such activity as) frightening sincerity
       (ii) sincerity is not the sort of thing that can be frightened
      (iii) one can(not) frighten sincerity

Clearly, a descriptively adequate grammar must indicate that (15) is deviant (as in the case of the examples of (10)) and that the examples of (16) are not. There are various ways to approach this problem.

Suppose that the selectional rules are included in the syntax. Then (15) and (16) are only derivatively generated by the grammar (in the sense of page 117, footnote); they are generated with Phrase-markers indicating that they depart in a particular respect from grammatical-ness. Since (15) nevertheless differs from (16) in 'deviance' from the intuitive point of view, this intuitive notion does not correspond to grammaticalness. Rather, it is presumably a property determined by the joint operation of both the syntactic and the semantic components. Thus the projection rules of the semantic component and the lexical entries for such words as *nonsense* and *speak* must be designed in such a way that, although the constitutent *frighten sincerity* of the generalized Phrase-markers of (16i–iii) is marked as semantically incongruous, the incongruity is removed by the readings assigned to constituents dominating it, and consequently the sentences (16) (but not (15)) are finally given a nondeviant interpretation. This seems to me not at all an unnatural or intolerable consequence. Surely it is not surprising to find that an intuitive concept such as 'deviance' can be explicated only in terms of theoretical constructs of various sorts, which have in them-selves no direct and uniform intuitive interpretation. In further support of this conclusion, one might cite the fact that even strict subcategoriza-tion rules can apparently be violated without leading necessarily to semantic incongruity, as, for example, in

(17) (i) it is nonsense to speak of (there is no such activity as)
         elapsing a book
     (ii) elapsing a book is not an activity that can be performed
     (iii) one cannot elapse a book

Here, too, one might plausibly maintain that base strings that deviate
significantly from grammaticalness are nevertheless constituents of
sentences that receive nondeviant interpretations, by virtue of the
semantic properties of certain lexical items and certain constructions.
In further support of the argument that grammaticalness cannot, in
any event, coincide with the intuitive notion of 'deviance', one can
cite cases of perfectly grammatical strings that are incongruous on
nonsyntactic grounds (cf. for example, p. 115).

Thus it seems to me that examples such as (16) do not present a
particularly strong argument for removing selectional rules from the
syntactic component and assigning their function to the interpretive
semantic rules. Nevertheless, if the latter course is taken, then (15) and
(16) will be directly generated by the syntactic rules, and at least in
such cases as these the relation of grammaticalness to intuitive deviance
will therefore be much closer. This might be cited as a slight consideration in favour of the decision to eliminate the selectional rules from the
syntactic component, and to modify the theory of the semantic component in some way so as to allow it to accommodate these phenomena.

We have been considering the possibility of assigning the function
of selectional rules to the semantic component. Alternatively, one might
raise the question whether the functions of the semantic component
as described earlier should not be taken over, *in toto*, by the generative
syntactic rules. More specifically, we may ask whether the cycle of
interpretive rules that assign readings to higher nodes (larger
constituents) of the underlying generalized Phrase-marker should not
be made to apply before some of the syntactic rules, so that the distinction between the two components is, in effect, obliterated. This notion,
which is by no means to be ruled out *a priori*, is explored by Bever and
Rosenbaum, who show that if it is adopted, the internal organization
of the syntactic component must be revised in several essential ways.

It is clear from this fragmentary and inconclusive discussion that the
interrelation of semantic and syntactic rules is by no means a settled
issue, and that there is quite a range of possibilities that deserve serious
exploration. The approach I have adopted is a conservative compro-
mise between the attempt to incorporate the semantic rules strictly
within the syntactic component and the attempt to elaborate the

semantic component so that it takes over the function of the selectional rules. Evidently, further insight into these questions will await a much more intensive study of semantic interpretive rules than it has yet been possible to undertake. The work of the last few years, I believe, has laid the groundwork for empirical investigation of this sort. There is a general theoretical framework parts of which have received empirical support. Within this framework it is possible to formulate certain reasonably clear questions, and it is also fairly clear what kind of empirical evidence would be relevant to deciding them. Alternative positions can be formulated, but for the present any one that is adopted must be extremely tentative.

In general, one should not expect to be able to delimit a large and complex domain before it has been thoroughly explored. A decision as to the boundary separating syntax and semantics (if there is one) is not a prerequisite for theoretical and descriptive study of syntactic and semantic rules. On the contrary, the problem of delimitation will clearly remain open until these fields are much better understood than they are today. Exactly the same can be said about the boundary separating semantic systems from systems of knowledge and belief. That these seem to interpenetrate in obscure ways has long been noted. One can hardly achieve significant understanding of this matter in advance of a deep analysis of systems of semantic rules, on the one hand, and systems of belief, on the other. Short of this, one can discuss only isolated examples within a theoretical vacuum. It is not surprising that nothing conclusive results from this.

5.6 *Some additional problems of semantic theory*

One major qualification must be added to this discussion of the relation of syntax to semantics. I have described the semantic component as a system of rules that assign readings to constituents of Phrase-markers—a system that has no intrinsic structure beyond this. But such a description is hardly sufficient. In particular, there is little doubt that the system of 'dictionary definitions' is not as atomistic as implied by this account.

Concerning dictionary definitions, two major problems are open to investigation. First, it is important to determine the universal, language-independent constraints on semantic features—in traditional terms, the system of possible concepts. The very notion 'lexical entry' presupposes some sort of fixed, universal vocabulary in terms of which these objects are characterized, just as the notion 'phonetic representa-

tion' presupposes some sort of universal phonetic theory. It is surely
our ignorance of the relevant psychological and physiological facts
that makes possible the widely-held belief that there is little or no *a
priori* structure to the system of 'attainable concepts'.

Furthermore, quite apart from the question of universal constraints,
it seems obvious that in any given linguistic system lexical entries
enter into intrinsic semantic relations of a much more systematic
sort than is suggested by what has been said so far. We might use the
term 'field properties' to refer to these undoubtedly significant though
poorly understood aspects of a descriptive semantic theory. Thus,
for example, consider Adjectives that are mutually exclusive in some
referential domain for example, colour words. Such 'antonymy sets'
(cf. Katz, 1964) provide a simple example of a field property that
cannot be described naturally in terms of separate lexical entries,
though it obviously plays a role in semantic interpretation. Or consider
the 'have a' relation, discussed in Bever and Rosenbaum. We have

(18)   (i)   the man has an arm
       (ii) the arm has a finger
       (iii) the finger has a cut

but not

(19)   (i)   the arm has a man
       (ii) the finger has an arm
       (iii) the cut has a finger

(except, irrelevantly to this point, as possible elliptic variants of
entirely different constructions, as in 'the finger has an arm attached
to it', 'the arm has a man on it', etc.). These examples, furthermore,
illustrate relations of meaning rather than relations of fact. Thus there
is no grammatical objection to 'the ant has a kidney', where 'the
kidney has an ant' is not false or impossible but senseless, with the
irrelevant exception just noted. In this case, we have a hierarchy of
terms with systematic relations that, once again, cannot in any natural
way be described within the framework of independent lexical entries.
Other systems of this sort can easily be found, and, in fact, they suggest
that part of the semantic component of a grammar must be a characterization of field properties that is outside the lexicon. This matter is
crucial but has been relatively unexplored within any general framework, though there have been several valuable studies of certain of its
aspects. Suppose, furthermore, that an attempt is made to relate

'deviance' in the intuitive sense to 'degree of grammaticalness' in the technical sense by excluding such examples as (19i–iii) from direct generation. The consequences of such a decision are not easy to determine.

Once again, we can do no more here than indicate problems and stress the fact that there are many unanswered questions of principle that might very well affect the formulation of even those parts of the theory of grammar that seem reasonably well established.

Finally, it is important to be aware of the many other problems that face a theory of semantic interpretation of the kind referred to in the preceding discussion. It is clear, as Katz and Fodor have emphasized, that the meaning of a sentence is based on the meaning of its elementary parts and the manner of their combination. It is also clear that the manner of combination provided by the surface (immediate constituent) structure is in general almost totally irrelevant to semantic interpretation, whereas the grammatical relations expressed in the abstract deep structure are, in many cases, just those that determine the meaning of the sentence. However, there are cases that suggest the need for an even more abstract notion of grammatical function and grammatical relation than any that has been developed so far, in any systematic way. Consider, for example, these sentence pairs:

(20) (i) John strikes me as pompous—I regard John as pompous
       (ii) I liked the play—the play pleased me
       (iii) John bought the book from Bill—Bill sold the book to John
       (iv) John struck Bill—Bill received a blow at the hands of John

Clearly, there is a meaning relation, approaching a variety of paraphrase, in these cases. It is not expressible in transformational terms, as is possible, for example, in these cases:

(21) (i) John is easy for us to please—it is easy for us to please John
       (ii) it was yesterday that he came—he came yesterday

In the case of (21), the deep structures of the paired sentences are identical in all respects relevant to semantic interpretation of the sort we are considering here, so that the transformational analysis accounts for the (cognitive) synonymy. This does not seem to be true in the case of (20), however. For example, in the case of (20i), although the deep structures would show that 'pompous' modifies 'John' in both sentences of the pair, they would not express the relations of the two Nouns to the Verb that are (in some unclear sense) the semantically significant ones. Thus in some sense the relation of 'John' to 'strike' is the same as that of 'John' to 'regard', and the relation of 'strike' to 'me' is the same as that of 'regard' to 'I'. We have no mechanism for expressing this fact, hence of accounting for the meaning relation, in terms of lexical features or grammatical relations of the deep structure. Consequently, it seems that beyond the notions of surface structure (such as 'grammatical subject') and deep structure (such as 'logical subject'), there is some still more abstract notion of 'semantic function' still unexplained. Various formal devices for expressing these facts suggest themselves, but the general problem seems to me nontrivial.

Many related problems have been raised in the extensive discussion of the distinction between the 'grammatical' Subject and Predicate of a sentence and its 'logical' or 'psychological' Subject and Predicate. To mention just one, Cook Wilson maintains (1926, pp. 119 f.) that 'in the statement "glass is elastic", if the matter of inquiry was elasticity and the question was what substances possessed the property of elasticity, glass . . . would no longer be subject, and the kind of stress which fell upon "elastic" when glass was the subject, would now be transferred to "glass" '. Thus in the statement '*glass* is elastic', ' "glass", which has the stress, is the only word which refers to the supposed new fact in the nature of elasticity, that it is found in glass . . . [and therefore] . . . "glass" would have to be the predicate . . . Thus the same form of words should be analysed differently according as the words are the answer to one question or another', and, in general, 'the subject and predicate are not necessarily *words* in the sentence, nor even something denoted by words in the sentence'. Whatever the force of such observations may be, it seems that they lie beyond the scope of any existing theory of language structure or language use.

To conclude this highly inconclusive discussion, I shall simply point out that the syntactic and semantic structure of natural languages evidently offers many mysteries, both of fact and of principle, and that any attempt to delimit the boundaries of these domains must certainly be quite tentative.

Aspects of the Theory of Syntax, 75–7, 148–54, 157–63

6 Language Acquisition

6.1 *Introductory*

[There would seem to be at least three reasons why research into children's acquisition of language is important.

(i) It is interesting in its own right.

(ii) The results of studies in language acquisition may throw light on a variety of educational and medical problems, e.g. aphasia, speech-retardation and cognitive development.

(iii) Since the study of language acquisition may confirm or disconfirm the universal categories postulated by linguistic theories with an explicitly mentalist basis, it is clear that the phenomena of language acquisition are relevant to the development of linguistic theory.

Many linguists and non-linguists have studied language acquisition without making any real effort to define how the results of their studies might be applied, and without wishing to prove anything about the nature of language. The result of this rather casual approach has been a mass of observations which inevitably tend to be of an anecdotal and therefore unsystematic nature. Moreover, the lack of any coherent theory of language acquisition means that the link between the data and what we assume to be the 'facts' of language acquisition are necessarily extremely tenuous. For example, it is difficult to describe, let alone explain, the facts of slow speech development without knowing precisely what constitutes normal speech development. Unfortunately we know very little at the present time about what constitutes normal speech development. This is due partly to the immense practical difficulties involved in studying child speech but also to the fact that there is no linguistic theory yet available which provides a sufficiently detailed apparatus to enable us either to describe the facts or to catalogue them comprehensively.

It may be useful, before turning to Chomsky's views on the subject, to give some indication of the practical and theoretical difficulties involved in studying language acquisition. Firstly, it is difficult for obvious practical reasons to study input-data, that is the amount and nature of speech to which the child is exposed over a period of two to three years (what Chomsky calls 'primary linguistic data'). It is clear that such studies are necessary if we wish, for example, to test Skinner's theory that language is learned by 'reinforcement', or to find out precisely what is learned by the child and what we must assume to be part of his innate capacity for acquiring language.

Secondly, it is difficult to study output-data, that is, to describe in precise grammatical terms the utterances that the child produces. Child speech is by its very nature structurally impoverished. Usually, and certainly in the earliest stages, we need a lot of situational (and phonological) information to determine the meaning of a child's utterances. For example, 'mummy chair' might mean 'that's mummy's chair' or 'mummy has a chair'. Should we be content simply to describe this utterance as a sequence of Noun+Noun or should we try to determine the nature of the underlying sentences, in order to describe the utterance as ambiguous?

Thirdly, it is difficult to study input-output relations. This is mainly due to the fact that there may be a considerable time-lag between what the child hears and what he produces.

Fourthly, it is extremely difficult to test the child's competence and to sort out performance variables. How do we know, for example, when a young child 'makes a mistake' in terms of his own system of competence? Children are notoriously difficult subjects to test.

Lastly, although it seems clear that the deep-surface distinction is valid for child-language it is not so clear what the exact relationship is between the deep component of an adult grammar and the deep component of a child grammar given, say, a base component of the type that Chomsky describes in *Aspects*. To illustrate this difficulty let us compare on the one hand the following synonymous set of child utterances: *juice, me juice, want juice, my juice* (all meaning: 'give me some juice' or 'I want some juice') and on the other hand the adult utterances *give me some juice. I want some juice.* Given this data, the researcher faces the following dilemma. If he assumes that an adult grammar and a child grammar share the same deep component, then the data is not describable in terms of a base component such as Chomsky provides in *Aspects*. In order to describe the data, a far more abstract universal deep component would be required. On the other hand, if the researcher assumes that an adult grammar and a child grammar do not share the same deep component, then the notion of substantive linguistic universals (see p. 140) is in danger of becoming incoherent.

It is probably true to say that for descriptive purposes most researchers in the field of language acquisition would favour the assumption that an adult grammar and a child grammar share the same deep component (most changes in 'transitional competence' could be conveniently stated in the transformational component of a standard grammar)—if only we had a well-developed linguistic theory based on this assumption, not to mention a theory based on *evidence* for such an assumption! [A, B]]

6.2 *Experimental approaches*

The attempt to write a grammar for a child raises all of the unsolved problems of constructing a grammar for adult speech, multiplied by some rather large factor. To mention just the most obvious difficulty, since the language is constantly changing rather dramatically, it is impossible to use the one 'method' available to linguists who attempt to go beyond surface description, namely learning the language oneself. Clearly the general problem is at least as difficult, and, in fact, much more difficult than the problem of discovering the grammar of the language of a mature speaker, and this, I think, is a problem of much greater difficulty than is often realized. In fact, the only remarks I would like to make reflect an impression that underlying these descriptions of children's speech*, laudable and interesting as they are, there is a somewhat oversimplified conception of the character of grammatical description, not unrelated, perhaps, to a similarly oversimplified view that is typical of much recent work on language in psychology and linguistics.

For one thing, it should be clearly recognized that a grammar is not a description of the performance of the speaker, but rather of his linguistic competence, and that a description of competence and a description of performance are different things. To illustrate, consider a trivial example where one would want to distinguish between a

* This paper was originally read at a Conference on First-Language Acquisition held at Endicott House, Dedham, Massachusetts, 27–29 October 1961, and contains comments on a paper by Wick Miller and Susan Ervin entitled 'The Development of Grammar in Child Language'. In this paper Miller and Ervin suggest that grammatical systems arise in the child's exposure to differing probabilities in adult speech and that the 'correct' patterns are reinforced, thus enabling the child to approximate adult patterns more closely. [A, B]

description of competence and a description of performance. Suppose that we were to attempt to give an account of how a child learns to multiply (rather than how he acquires his language). A child who has succeeded in learning this has acquired a certain competence, and he will perform in certain ways that are clearly at variance with this competence. Once he has learned to multiply, the correct description of his competence is a statement, in one or another form of some of the rules of arithmetic—i.e. a specification of the set of triples (x, y, z) such that z is the product of x and y. On the other hand, a description of the performance of either an adult or a child (or a real computer) would be something quite different. It might, for example, be a specification of a set of quadruples (x, y, z, w) such that w is the probability that, given x and y, the person will compute the product as z. This set of quadruples would incorporate information about memory span, characteristic errors, lapses of attention, etc., information which is relevant to a performance table but not, clearly, to an account of what the person has learned—what is the basic competence that he has acquired. A person might memorize the performance table and perform on various simple-minded tests exactly as the person who knows the rules of arithmetic but this would not, of course, show that he knows these rules. It seems clear that the description which is of greatest psychological relevance is the account of competence, not that of performance, both in the case of arithmetic and the case of language. The deeper question concerns the kinds of structures the person has succeeded in mastering and internalizing, whether or not he utilizes them, in practice, without interference from the many other factors that play a role in actual behaviour. For anyone concerned with intellectual processes, or any question that goes beyond mere data arranging, it is the question of competence that is fundamental. Obviously one can find out about competence only by studying performance, but this study must be carried out in devious and clever ways, if any serious result is to be obtained.

These rather obvious comments apply directly to study of language, child or adult. Thus it is absurd to attempt to construct a grammar that describes observed linguistic behaviour directly. The tape-recordings of this conference give a totally false picture of the conceptions of linguistic structure of the various speakers. Nor is this in the least bit surprising. The speaker has represented in his brain a grammar that gives an ideal account of the structure of the sentences of his language, but, when actually faced with the task of speaking or 'understanding', many other factors act upon his underlying linguistic competence to produce actual performance. He may be confused or have several things in mind, change his plans in midstream, etc. Since this is obviously the condition of most actual linguistic perforance, a direct record—an actual corpus—is almost useless as it stands, for linguistic analysis of any but the most superficial kind.

Similarly, it seems to me that, if anything far-reaching and real is to be discovered about the actual grammar of the child, then rather devious kinds of observations of his performance, his abilities, and his comprehension in many different kinds of circumstance will have to be obtained, so that a variety of evidence may be brought to bear on the attempt to determine what is in fact his underlying linguistic competence at each stage of development. Direct description of the child's actual verbal output is no more likely to provide an account of the real underlying competence in the case of child language than in the case of adult language, ability to multiply, or any other nontrivial rule-governed behaviour. Not that one shouldn't start here, perhaps, but surely one shouldn't end here, or take too seriously the results obtained by one or another sort of manipulation of data of texts produced under normal conditions.

It is suggested in this paper—and this is a view shared by many psychologists and linguists—that the relation between competence and performance is somehow a probabilistic one. That is, somehow the higher probabilities in actual output converge towards the actual underlying grammar, or something of the sort. I have never seen a coherent presentation of this position, but, even as a vague idea, it seems to me entirely implausible. In particular, it surely cannot be maintained that the child forms his conceptions of grammatical structure by just assuming that high probabilities correspond to 'rules' and that low probabilities can be disregarded, in some manner. Most of what the child actually produces and hears (and this is true for the adult as well) is of extremely low probability. In fact, in the case of sentence structure, the notion of probability loses all meaning. Except for a ridiculously small number (e.g. conventionalized greetings, etc., which, in fact, often do not even observe grammatical rules), all actual sentences are of a probability so low as to be effectively zero, and the same is true of structures (if, by the 'structure' of a sentence, we mean the sequence of categories to which its successive words or morphemes belong). In actual speech, the highest probability must be assigned to broken and interrupted fragments of sentences or to sentences which begin in one way and end in a different, totally incompatible way (surely the tapes of this meeting would be sufficient to demonstrate this). From such evidence it would be absurd to conclude that this represents in any sense the linguistic consciousness of the speakers, as has been noted above. In general, it is a mistake to assume that—past the very earliest stages—much of what the child acquires is acquired by imitation. This could not be true on the level of sentence formation, since most of what the child hears is new and most of what he produces, past the very earliest stages, is new.

In the papers that have been presented here—and again, this is not unrepresentative of psychology and linguistics—there has been talk about grammars for the decoder and grammars for the encoder. Again, there are several undemonstrated (and, to me, quite implausible) assumptions underlying the view that the speaker's behaviour should be modelled by one sort of system, and the hearer's by another. I have never seen a precise characterization of a 'grammar for the encoder' or a 'grammar for the decoder' that was not convertible, by a notational change, into the other. Furthermore, this is not surprising. The grammars that linguists construct are, in fact, quite neutral as between speaker and hearer. The problems of constructing models of performance, for the speaker and hearer, incorporating these grammars, are rather similar. This, of course, bears again on the question of relation between competence and performance. That is, the grammar that represents the speaker's competence is, of course, involved in both his speaking and interpreting of speech, and there seems no reason to assume that there are two different underlying systems, one involved in speaking, one in 'understanding'. To gain some insight into this underlying system, studies of the speaker's actual output, as well as of his ability to understand and interpret, are essential. But again, it cannot be too strongly emphasized that the data obtained in such studies can only serve as the grounds for inference about what constitutes the linguistic consciousness that provides the basis for language use.

A few other minor remarks of this sort might be made to indicate areas in which experimental methods that go far beyond mere observation of speech in normal situations will be needed to shed some light on underlying competence. To take just one example, it is often remarked, and, in particular, it is remarked in this paper, that in the case of lexical items (as distinct from 'function words', so-called) it is generally possible to assign referential meaning rather easily. Of course, as clearly stated in the paper, this is in part a matter of degree.

However, I think that the notion that it is generally a straightforward matter in the case of lexical items is a faulty conclusion derived from concentration on atypical examples. Perhaps in the case of 'green', 'table', etc., it is not difficult to determine what is the 'referential meaning'. But consider, on the other hand, such words as 'useful', where the meaning is clearly 'relational'—the things in the world cannot be divided into those that are useful and those that are not. In fact, the meaning of 'useful', like that of a function word, in some respects, must be described in partly relational terms. Or, to take a more complicated example, consider a word like 'expect'. A brief attempt to prescribe the behaviours or situations that make application of this word appropriate will quickly convince one that this is entirely the wrong approach and that 'referential meaning' is simply the wrong concept in this case. I don't think that such examples are at all exotic. It may be that such atypical examples as 'table' and 'green' are relatively more frequent in the early stages of language learning (though this remains to be shown, just as it remains to be shown that determination of referential meaning in such cases is in some sense 'primitive'), and, if true, this may be important. However, this is clearly not going to carry one very far.

Consider now a rather comparable phonetic example. One of the problems to be faced is that of characterizing the child's phonemic system. Phonemes are often defined by linguists as constituting a family of mutually exclusive classes of phones, and this is the definition adopted in this paper. If this were true, there would be, in this case, a fairly simple relation between performance (i.e. a sequence of phones) and the underlying abstract system (i.e. the phonemic representation of this sequence). One might hope that by some simple classification technique one might determine the phonemic system from the phonetic record or the phonemic constitution of an utterance from the sequence of its phones. There is, however, extremely strong evidence (so it seems to me, at least) that phonemes cannot be defined as classes of sounds at all (and certainly not as mutually exclusive classes) and that the relation between a phonemic system and the phonetic record (just as the relation between a phonemic representation of an utterance and its actual sound) is much more remote and complex.

These two examples are randomly chosen illustrations of a general tendency to oversimplify drastically the facts of linguistic structure and to assume that the determination of competence can be derived from description of a corpus by some sort of sufficiently developed data-processing techniques. My feeling is that this is hopeless and that only experimentation of a fairly indirect and ingenious sort can provide evidence that is at all critical for formulating a true account of the child's grammar (as in the case of investigation of any other real system). Consequently, I would hope that some of the research in this area would be diverted from recording of texts towards attempting to tap the child's underlying abilities to use and comprehend sentences, to detect deviance and compensate for it, to apply rules in new situations, to form highly specific concepts from scattered bits of evidence, and so on. There are, after all, many ways in which such study can be approached. Thus, for example, the child's ability to repeat sentences and nonsentences, phonologically possible sequences and phonologically impossible ones, etc., might provide some evidence as to the underlying system that he is using. There is surely no doubt that the child's achievements in systematizing linguistic data, at every stage, go well beyond what he actually produces in normal speech. Thus it is striking that advances are generally 'across the board'. A child who does not produce initial s + consonant clusters may begin to produce them all, at approximately the same time, thus distinguishing for the first time between 'cool' and 'school', etc.—but characteristically will do this in just the right words, indicating that the correct phonemic representation of these words was present to the mind even at the stage where it did not appear in speech. Similarly, some of the data of Brown and Fraser seem to suggest that interrogatives, negatives, and other syntactically related forms appear and are distinguished from declaratives at approximately the same time, for some children. If so, this suggests that what has actually happened is that the hitherto latent system of verbal auxiliaries is now no longer suppressed in actual speech, as previously. Again, this can be investigated directly. Thus a child producing speech in a 'telegraphic style' can be shown to have an underlying, fuller conception of sentence structure (unrealized in his speech, but actively involved in comprehension) if misplacement of the elements he does not produce leads to difficulties of comprehension, inability to repeat, etc., while correct placement gives utterances intelligible to him, and so on.

'Formal discussion' in *The Acquisition of Language*,
Bellugi and Brown (1964)

6.3 *Rationalist and empiricist views*

Applying a rationalist view to the special case of language learning, Humboldt (1836) concludes that one cannot really teach language but can only present the conditions under which it will develop spontaneously in the mind in its own way. Thus the *form of a language*, the schema for its grammar, is to a large extent given, though it will not be available for use without appropriate experience to set the language-forming processes into operation. Like Leibniz, he reiterates the Platonistic view that, for the individual, learning is largely a matter of *Wiedererzeugung*, that is, of drawing out what is innate in the mind.

This view contrasts sharply with the empiricist notion (the prevailing modern view) that language is essentially an adventitious construct, taught by 'conditioning' (as would be maintained, for example, by Skinner or Quine) or by drill and explicit explanation (as was claimed by Wittgenstein), or built up by elementary 'data-processing' procedures (as modern linguistics typically maintains), but, in any event, relatively independent in its structure of any innate mental faculties.

In short, empiricist speculation has characteristically assumed that only the procedures and mechanisms for the acquisition of knowledge constitute an innate property of the mind. Thus for Hume, the method of 'experimental reasoning' is a basic instinct in animals and humans, on a par with the instinct 'which teaches a bird, with such exactness, the art of incubation, and the whole economy and order of its nursery'— it is derived 'from the original hand of nature' (Hume, 1748, § IX). The form of knowledge, however, is otherwise quite free. On the other hand, rationalist speculation has assumed that the general form of a system of knowledge is fixed in advance as a disposition of the mind, and the function of experience is to cause this general schematic structure to be realized and more fully differentiated. To follow Leibniz's enlightening analogy, we may make

'. . . the comparison of a block of marble which has veins, rather than a block of marble wholly even, or of blank tablets, i.e. of what is called among philosophers a *tabula rasa*. For if the soul resembled these blank tablets, truths would be in us as the figure of Hercules is in the marble, when the marble is wholly indifferent to the reception of this figure or some other. But if there were veins in the block which would indicate the figure of Hercules rather than other figures, this block would be more determined thereto, and Hercules would be in it as in some sense innate, although it would be needful to labour to discover these veins, to clear them by polishing, and by cutting away what prevents them from appearing. Thus it is that ideas and truths are for us innate, as inclinations, dispositions, habits, or natural potentialities, and not as actions; although these potentialities are always accompanied by some actions, often insensible, which correspond to them' [Leibniz, *New Essays*, pp. 45–6].

It is not, of course, necessary to assume that empiricist and rationalist views can always be sharply distinguished and that these currents cannot cross. Nevertheless, it is historically accurate as well as heuristically valuable to distinguish these two very different approaches to the problem of acquisition of knowledge. Particular empiricist and rationalist views can be made quite precise and can then be presented as explicit hypotheses about acquisition of knowledge, in particular, about the innate structure of a language-acquisition device. In fact, it would not be inaccurate to describe the taxonomic, data-processing approach of modern linguistics as an empiricist view that contrasts with the essentially rationalist alternative proposed in recent theories of transformational grammar. Taxonomic linguistics is empiricist in its assumption that general linguistic theory consists only of a body of procedures for determining the grammar of a language from a corpus of data, the form of language being unspecified except in so far as restrictions on possible grammars are determined by this set of procedures. If we interpret taxonomic linguistics as making an empirical claim, this claim must be that the grammars that result from application of the postulated procedures to a sufficiently rich selection of data will be descriptively adequate—in other words, that the set of procedures can be regarded as constituting a hypothesis about the innate language-acquisition system. In contrast, the discussion of language acquisition in preceding sections was rationalistic in its assumption that various formal and substantive universals are intrinsic properties of the language-acquisition system, these providing a schema that is applied to data and that determines in a highly restricted way the general form and, in part, even the substantive features of the grammar that may emerge upon presentation of appropriate data. A general linguistic theory of the sort roughly described earlier, and elaborated in more detail in the following chapters and in other studies of transformational grammar, must therefore be regarded as a specific hypothesis, of an essentially rationalist cast, as to the nature of mental structures and processes.

Aspects of the Theory of Syntax, 51–3

6.4 *Criticism of reinforcement theory*

It is a common observation that a young child of immigrant parents may learn a second language in the streets, from other children, with amazing rapidity, and that his speech may be completely fluent and correct to the last allophone, while the subtleties that become second nature to the child may elude his parents despite high motivation and continued practice. A child may pick up a large part of his vocabulary and 'feel' for sentence structure from television, from reading, from listening to adults, etc. Even a very young child who has not yet acquired a minimal repertoire from which to form new utterances may imitate a word quite well on an early try, with no attempt on the part of his parents to teach it to him. It is also perfectly obvious that, at a later stage, a child will be able to construct and understand utterances which are quite new, and are, at the same time, acceptable sentences in his language. Every time an adult reads a newspaper, he undoubtedly comes upon countless new sentences which are not at all similar, in a simple, physical sense, to any that he has heard before, and which he will recognize as sentences and understand; he will also be able to detect slight distortions or misprints. Talk of 'stimulus generalization' in such a case simply perpetuates the mystery under a new title. These abilities indicate that there must be fundamental processes at work quite independently of 'feedback' from the environment. I have been able to find no support whatsoever for the doctrine of Skinner and others that slow and careful shaping of verbal behaviour through differential reinforcement is an absolute necessity. If reinforcement theory really requires the assumption that there be such meticulous care, it seems best to regard this simply as a *reductio ad absurdum* argument against this approach. It is also not easy to find any basis (or, for that matter, to attach very much content) to the claim that reinforcing contingencies set up by the verbal community are the single factor responsible for maintaining the strength of verbal behaviour. The sources of the 'strength' of this behaviour are almost a total mystery at present. Reinforcement undoubtedly plays a significant role, but so do a variety of motivational factors about which nothing serious is known in the case of human beings.

As far as acquisition of language is concerned, it seems clear that reinforcement, casual observation, and natural inquisitiveness (coupled with a strong tendency to imitate) are important factors, as is the remarkable capacity of the child to generalize, hypothesize, and 'process information' in a variety of very special and apparently highly complex ways which we cannot yet describe or begin to understand, and which may be largely innate, or may develop through some sort of learning or through maturation of the nervous system. The manner in which such factors operate and interact in language acquisition is completely unknown. It is clear that what is necessary in such a case is research, not dogmatic and perfectly arbitrary claims based on analogies to that small part of the experimental literature in which one happens to be interested.

The pointlessness of these claims becomes clear when we consider the well-known difficulties in determining to what extent inborn structure, maturation, and learning are responsible for the particular form of a skilled or complex performance. To take just one example, the gaping response of a nestling thrush is at first released by jarring of the nest, and, at a later stage, by a moving object of specific size, shape, and position relative to the nestling. At this later stage the response is directed towards the part of the stimulus object corresponding to the parent's head, and characterized by a complex configuration of stimuli that can be precisely described. Knowing just this, it would be possible to construct a speculative, learning-theoretic account of how this sequence of behaviour patterns might have developed through a process of differential reinforcement, and it would no doubt be possible to train rats to do something similar. However, there appears to be good evidence that these responses to fairly complex 'sign stimuli' are genetically determined and mature without learning. Clearly, the possibility cannot be discounted. Consider now the comparable case of a child imitating new words. At an early stage we may find rather gross correspondences. At a later stage, we find that repetition is, of course, far from exact (i.e. it is not mimicry, a fact which itself is interesting), but that it reproduces the highly complex configuration of sound features that constitute the phonological structure of the language in question. Again, we can propose a speculative account of how this result might have been obtained through elaborate arrangement of reinforcing contingencies. Here too, however, it is possible that ability to select out of the complex auditory input those features that are phonologically relevant may develop largely independently of reinforcement, through genetically determined maturation. To the extent that this is true, an account of the development and causation of behaviour that fails to consider the structure of the organism will provide no understanding of the real processes involved.

It is often argued that experience, rather than innate capacity to handle information in certain specific ways, must be the factor of overwhelming dominance in determining the specific character of language acquisition since a child speaks the language of the group in which he lives. But this is a superficial argument. As long as we are speculating, we may consider the possibility that the brain has evolved to the point where, given an input of observed Chinese sentences, it produces (by an 'induction' of apparently fantastic complexity and suddenness) the 'rules' of Chinese grammar, and given an input of observed English sentences, it produces (by, perhaps, exactly the same process of induction) the rules of English grammar; or that given an observed application of a term to certain instances it automatically predicts the extension to a class of complexly related instances. If clearly recognized as such, this speculation is neither unreasonable nor fantastic; nor, for that matter, is it beyond the bounds of possible study. There is, of course, no known neural structure capable of performing this task in the specific ways that observation of the resulting behaviour might lead us to postulate; but for that matter, the structures capable of accounting for even the simplest kinds of learning have similarly defied detection.

Summarizing this brief discussion, it seems that there is neither empirical evidence nor any known argument to support any specific claim about the relative importance of 'feedback' from the environment and the 'independent contribution of the organism' in the process of language acquisition.

A Review of B. F. Skinner's Verbal Behavior (*1959*), *42–4*

6.5 *Formal and substantive universals*

A theory of linguistic structure that aims for explanatory adequacy incorporates an account of linguistic universals, and it attributes tacit knowledge of these universals to the child. It proposes, then, that the child approaches the data with the presumption that they are drawn from a language of a certain antecedently well-defined type, his problem being to determine which of the (humanly) possible languages is that of the community in which he is placed. Language learning would be impossible unless this were the case. The important question is: What are the initial assumptions concerning the nature of language that the child brings to language learning, and how detailed and specific is the innate schema (the general definition of 'grammar') that gradually becomes more explicit and differentiated as the child learns the language? For the present we cannot come at all close to making a hypothesis about innate schemata that is rich, detailed, and specific enough to account for the fact of language acquisition. Consequently, the main task of linguistic theory must be to develop an account of linguistic universals that, on the one hand, will not be falsified by the actual diversity of languages and, on the other will be sufficiently rich and explicit to account for the rapidity and uniformity of language learning, and the remarkable complexity and range of the generative grammars that are the product of language learning.

The study of linguistic universals is the study of the properties of any generative grammar for a natural language. Particular assumptions about linguistic universals may pertain to either the syntactic, semantic, or phonological component, or to interrelations among the three components.

It is useful to classify linguistic universals as *formal* or *substantive*. A theory of substantive universals claims that items of a particular kind in any language must be drawn from a fixed class of items. For example, Jakobson's theory of distinctive features can be interpreted as making an assertion about substantive universals with respect to the phonological component of a generative grammar. It asserts that each output of this component consists of elements that are characterized in terms of some small number of fixed universal, phonetic features, each of which has a substantive acoustic-articulatory characterization independent of any particular language. Traditional universal grammar was also a theory of substantive universals, in this sense. It not only put forth interesting views as to the nature of universal phonetics, but also advanced the position that certain fixed syntactic categories (Noun, Verb, etc.) can be found in the syntactic representations of the sentences of any language and that these provide the general underlying syntactic structure of each language. A theory of substantive semantic universals might hold for example, that certain designative functions must be carried out in a specified way in each language. Thus it might assert that each language will contain terms that designate persons or lexical items referring to certain specific kinds of objects, feelings, behaviour, and so on.

It is also possible, however, to search for universal properties of a more abstract sort. Consider a claim that the grammar of every language meets certain specified formal conditions. The truth of this hypothesis would not in itself imply that any particular rule must appear in all or even in any two grammars. The property of having a grammar meeting a certain abstract condition might be called a *formal* linguistic universal, if shown to be a general property of natural languages. Recent attempts to specify the abstract conditions that a generative grammar must meet have produced a variety of proposals concerning formal universals, in this sense. For example, consider the proposal that the syntactic component of a grammar must contain transformational rules (these being operations of a highly special kind) mapping semantically interpreted deep structures into phonetically interpreted surface structures, or the proposal that the phonological component of a grammar consists of a sequence of rules, a subset of which may apply cyclically to successively more dominant constituents of the surface structure (a transformational cycle, in the sense of much recent work on phonology). Such proposals make claims of a quite different sort from the claim that certain substantive phonetic elements are available for phonetic representation in all languages, or that certain specific categories must be central to the syntax of all languages, or that certain semantic features or categories provide a universal framework for semantic description. Substantive universals such as these concern the vocabulary for the description of language; formal universals involve rather the character of the rules that appear in grammars and the ways in which they can be interconnected.

On the semantic level, too, it is possible to search for what might be called formal universals, in essentially the sense just described. Consider, for example, the assumption that proper names, in any language, must designate objects meeting a condition of spatiotemporal contiguity, and that the same is true of other terms designating objects; or the condition that the colour words of any language must subdivide the colour spectrum into continuous segments; or the condition that artifacts are defined in terms of certain human goals, needs, and functions instead of solely in terms of physical qualities. Formal constraints of this sort on a system of concepts may severely limit the choice (by the child, or the linguist) of a descriptive grammar, given primary linguistic data.

The existence of deep-seated formal universals, in the sense suggested by such examples as these, implies that all languages are cut to the same pattern, but does not imply that there is any point by point correspondence between particular languages. It does not, for example, imply that there must be some reasonable procedure for translating between languages*.

---

* By a 'reasonable procedure' I mean one that does not involve extralinguistic information—that is, one that does not incorporate an 'encyclopedia'. The possibility of a reasonable procedure for translation between arbitrary languages depends on the sufficiency of substantive universals. In fact, although there is much reason to believe that languages are to a significant extent cast in the same mould, there is little reason to suppose that reasonable procedures of translation are in general possible. [C]

In general, there is no doubt that a theory of language, regarded as a hypothesis about the innate 'language-forming capacity' of humans, should concern itself with both substantive and formal universals. But whereas substantive universals have been the traditional concern of general linguistic theory, investigations of the abstract conditions that must be satisfied by any generative grammar have been undertaken only quite recently. They seem to offer extremely rich and varied possibilities for study in all aspects of grammar.

6.6 *Descriptive and explanatory theories*

Let us consider with somewhat greater care just what is involved in the construction of an 'acquisition model' for language. A child who is capable of language learning must have

(1) (i)   a technique for representing input signals
      (ii) a way of representing structural information about these signals
      (iii) some initial delimitation of a class of possible hypotheses about language structure
      (iv) a method for determining what each such hypothesis implies with respect to each sentence
      (v)   a method for selecting one of the (presumably, infinitely many) hypotheses that are allowed by (iii) and are compatible with the given primary linguistic data.

Correspondingly, a theory of linguistic structure that aims for explanatory adequacy must contain

(2) (i)   a universal phonetic theory that defines the notion 'possible sentence'
      (ii) a definition of 'structural description'
      (iii) a definition of 'generative grammar'
      (iv) a method for determining the structural description of a sentence, given a grammar
      (v)   a way of evaluating alternative proposed grammars

A theory meeting these conditions would attempt to account for language learning in the following way. Consider first the nature of primary linguistic data. This consists of a finite amount of information about sentences, which, furthermore, must be rather restricted in scope, considering the time limitations that are in effect, and fairly degenerate in quality. For example, certain signals might be accepted as properly formed sentences, while others are classed as nonsentences, as a result of correction of the learners' attempts on the part of linguistic community. Furthermore, the conditions of use might be such as to require that structural descriptions be assigned to these objects in certain ways. That the latter is a prerequisite for language acquisition seems to follow from the widely accepted (but, for the moment, quite unsupported) view that there must be a partially semantic basis for the acquisition of syntax or for the justification of hypotheses about the syntactic component of a grammar. Incidentally, it is often not realized how strong a claim this is about the innate concept-forming abilities of the child and the system of linguistic universals that these abilities imply. Thus what is maintained, presumably, is that the child has an innate theory of potential structural descriptions that is sufficiently rich and fully developed so that he is able to determine, from a real situation in which a signal occurs, which structural descriptions may be appropriate to this signal, and also that he is able to do this in part in advance of any assumption as to the linguistic structure of this signal. To say that the assumption about innate capacity is extremely strong is, of course, not to say that it is incorrect. Let us, in any event, assume tentatively that the primary linguistic data consists of signals classified as sentences and nonsentences, and a partial and tentative pairing of signals with structural descriptions.

A language-acquisition device that meets conditions (i)--(iv) is capable of utilizing such primary linguistic data as the empirical basis for language learning. This device must search through the set of possible hypotheses G_1, G_2, . . . , which are available to it by virtue of condition (iii), and must select grammars that are compatible with the primary linguistic data, represented in terms of (i) and (ii). It is possible to test compatibility by virtue of the fact that the device meets condition (iv). The device would then select one of these potential grammars by the evaluation measure guaranteed by (v). The selected grammar now provides the device with a method for interpreting an arbitrary sentence, by virtue of (ii) and (iv). That is to say, the device has now constructed a theory of the language of which the primary linguistic data are a sample. The theory that the device has now selected and internally represented specifies its tacit competence, its knowledge of the language. The child who acquires a language in this way, of course, knows a great deal more than he has 'learned'. His knowledge of the language, as this is determined by his internalized grammar, goes far beyond the presented primary linguistic data and is in no sense an 'inductive generalization' from these data.

This account of language learning can, obviously, be paraphrased directly as a description of how the linguist whose work is guided by a linguistic theory meeting conditions (i)–(v) would justify a grammar that he constructs for a language on the basis of given primary linguistic data.

Notice, incidentally, that care must be taken to distinguish several different ways in which primary linguistic data may be necessary for language learning. In part, such data determine to which of the possible languages (that is, the languages provided with grammars in accordance with the *a priori* constraint (iii)) the language learner is being exposed, and it is this function of the primary linguistic data that we are considering here. But such data may play an entirely different role as well; namely, certain kinds of data and experience may be required in order to set the language-acquisition device into operation, although they may not effect the manner of its functioning in the least. Thus it has been found that semantic reference may greatly facilitate performance in a syntax-learning experiment, even though it does not, apparently, effect the *manner* in which acquisition of syntax proceeds; that is, it plays no role in determining which hypotheses are selected by the learner (Miller and Norman, 1964). Similarly, it would not be at all surprising to find that normal language learning requires use of language in real-life situations, in some way. But this, if true, would not be sufficient to show that information regarding situational context (in particular, a pairing of signals with structural descriptions that is at least in part prior to assumptions about syntactic structure) plays any role in determining how language is acquired, once the mechanism is put to work and the task of language learning is undertaken by the child. This distinction is quite familiar outside of the domain of language acquisition. For example, Richard Held has shown in numerous experiments that under certain circumstances reafferent stimulation (that is stimulation resulting from voluntary activity) is a prerequisite to the development of a concept of visual space, although it may not determine the character of this concept (cf. Held and Hein, 1963; Held and Freedman, 1963, and references cited there). Or, to take one of innumerable examples from studies of animal learning, it has been observed (Lemmon and Patterson, 1964) that depth perception in lambs is considerably facilitated by mother-neonate contact, although again there is no reason to suppose that the nature of the lamb's 'theory of visual space' depends on this contact.

In studying the actual character of learning, linguistic or otherwise, it is, of course, necessary to distinguish carefully between these two functions of external data—the function of initiating or facilitating the operation of innate mechanisms and the function of determining in part the direction that learning will take.

Returning now to the main theme, we call a theory of linguistic structure that meets conditions (i)–(v) an *explanatory theory*, and a theory that meets conditions (i)–(iv) a *descriptive theory*. In fact, a linguistic theory that is concerned only with descriptive adequacy will limit its attention to topics (i)–(iv). Such a theory must, in other words, make available a class of generative grammars containing, for each language, a descriptively adequate grammar of this language—a grammar that (by means of (iv)) assigns structural descriptions to sentences in accordance with the linguistic competence of the native speaker. A theory of language is empirically significant only to the extent that it meets conditions (i)–(iv). The further question of explanatory adequacy arises in connection with a theory that also meets condition (v). In other words, it arises only to the extent that the theory provides a principled basis for selecting a descriptively adequate grammar on the basis of primary linguistic data by the use of a well-defined evaluation measure.

This account is misleading in one important respect. It suggests that to raise a descriptively adequate theory to the level of explanatory adequacy one needs only to define an appropriate evaluation measure. This is incorrect, however. A theory may be descriptively adequate, in the sense just defined, and yet provide such a wide range of potential grammars that there is no possibility of discovering a formal property distinguishing the descriptively adequate grammars, in general, from among the mass of grammars compatible with whatever data are available. In fact, the real problem is almost always to restrict the range of possible hypotheses by adding additional structure to the notion 'generative grammar'. For the construction of a reasonable acquisition model, it is necessary to reduce the class of attainable grammars compatible with given primary linguistic data to the point where selection among them can be made by a formal evaluation measure. This requires a precise and narrow delimitation of the notion 'generative grammar'—a restrictive and rich hypothesis concerning the universal properties that determine the form of language, in the traditional sense of this term.

The same point can be put in a somewhat different way. Given a variety of descriptively adequate grammars for natural languages, we are interested in determining to what extent they are unique and to what extent there are deep underlying similarities among them that are attributable to the form of language as such. Real progress in linguistics consists in the discovery that certain features of given languages can be reduced to universal properties of language, and explained in terms of these deeper aspects of linguistic form. Thus the major endeavour of the linguist must be to enrich the theory of linguistic form by formulating more specific constraints and conditions on the notion 'generative grammar'. Where this can be done, particular grammars can be simplified by eliminating from them descriptive statements that are attributable to the general theory of grammar. For example, if we conclude that the transformational cycle is a universal feature of the phonological component, it is unnecessary, in the grammar of English, to describe the manner of functioning of those phonological rules that involve syntactic structure. This description will now have been abstracted from the grammar of English and stated as a formal linguistic universal, as part of the theory of generative grammar. Obviously, this conclusion, if justified, would represent an important advance in the theory of language, since it would then have been shown that what appears to be a peculiarity of English is actually explicable in terms of a general and deep empirical assumption about the nature of language, an assumption that can be refuted, if false, by study of descriptively adequate grammars of other languages.

In short, the most serious problem that arises in the attempt to achieve explanatory adequacy is that of characterizing the notion 'generative grammar' in a sufficiently rich, detailed, and highly structured way. A theory of grammar may be descriptively adequate and yet leave unexpressed major features that are defining properties of natural language and that distinguish natural languages from arbitrary symbolic systems. It is for just this reason that the attempt to achieve explanatory adequacy—the attempt to discover linguistic universals—is so crucial at every stage of understanding of linguistic structure, despite the fact that even descriptive adequacy on a broad scale may be an unrealized goal. It is not necessary to achieve descriptive adequacy before raising questions of explanatory adequacy. On the contrary, the crucial questions, the questions that have the greatest bearing on our concept of language and on descriptive practice as well, are almost always those involving explanatory adequacy with respect to particular aspects of language structure.

To acquire language, a child must devise a hypothesis compatible with presented data—he must select from the store of potential grammars a specific one that is appropriate to the data available to him. It is logically possible that the data might be sufficiently rich and the class of potential grammars sufficiently limited so that no more than a single permitted grammar will be compatible with the available data at the moment of successful language acquisition, in our idealized 'instantaneous' model. In this case, no evaluation procedure will be necessary as a part of linguistic theory—that is, as an innate property of an organism or a device capable of language acquisition. It is rather difficult to imagine how in detail this logical possibility might be realized, and all concrete attempts to formulate an empirically adequate linguistic theory certainly leave ample room for mutually inconsistent grammars, all compatible with primary data of any conceivable sort. All such theories therefore require supplementation by an evaluation measure if language acquisition is to be accounted for and selection of specific grammars is to be justified; and I shall continue to assume tentatively, as heretofore, that this is an empirical fact about the innate human *faculté de langage* and consequently about general linguistic theory as well.

Aspects of the Theory of Syntax, 27–37

6.7 *Conclusion*

The child who learns a language has in some sense constructed the grammar for himself on the basis of his observation of sentences and nonsentences (i.e. corrections by the verbal community). Study of the actual observed ability of a speaker to distinguish sentences from nonsentences, detect ambiguities, etc., apparently forces us to the conclusion that this grammar is of an extremely complex and abstract character, and that the young child has succeeded in carrying out what from the formal point of view, at least, seems to be a remarkable type of theory construction. Furthermore, this task is accomplished in an astonishingly short time, to a large extent independently of intelligence, and in a comparable way by all children. Any theory of learning must cope with these facts.

It is not easy to accept the view that a child is capable of constructing an extremely complex mechanism for generating a set of sentences, some of which he has heard, or that an adult can instantaneously determine whether (and if so, how) a particular item is generated by this mechanism, which has many of the properties of an abstract deductive theory. Yet this appears to be a fair description of the performance of the speaker, listener, and learner. If this is correct, we can predict that a direct attempt to account for the actual behaviour of speaker, listener, and learner, not based on a prior understanding of the structure of grammars, will achieve very limited success. The grammar must be regarded as a component in the behaviour of the speaker and listener which can only be inferred, as Lashley has put it, from the resulting physical acts. The fact that all normal children acquire essentially comparable grammars of great complexity with remarkable rapidity suggests that human beings are somehow specially designed to do this, with data-handling or 'hypothesis-formulating' ability of unknown character and complexity. The study of linguistic structure may ultimately lead to some significant insights into this matter. At the moment the question cannot be seriously posed, but in principle it may be possible to study the problem of determining what the built-in structure of an information-processing (hypothesis-forming) system must be to enable it to arrive at the grammar of a language from the available data in the available time. At any rate, just as the attempt to eliminate the contribution of the speaker leads to a 'mentalistic' descriptive system that succeeds only in blurring important traditional distinctions, a refusal to study the contribution of the child to language learning permits only a superficial account of language acquisition, with a vast and unanalysed contribution attributed to a step called 'generalization' which in fact includes just about everything of interest in this process. If the study of language is limited in these ways, it seems inevitable that major aspects of verbal behaviour will remain a mystery.

A Review of B. F. Skinner's Verbal Behavior (1959), 57–8

7 Language Teaching

7.1 *Introductory*

[In recent years the methods employed in the foreign-language class-room have been heavily influenced by a combination of associative learning theory and taxonomic linguistics. As a result there has been a tendency to treat language as an inventory of elements or a collection of learned patterns. Mother-tongue teachers, following an older tradition, have attempted to induce a 'creative' use of language in their students, but without any serious attempt to discover what sort of linguistic knowledge a student needs in order to use his language successfully. Given this background, Chomsky's work in the field of psychology and linguistics has far-reaching implications for both L_1 and L_2 teaching, especially his insistence on the fact that human language is essentially innovative and stimulus-free, and his strong claim about the nature of the underlying linguistic knowledge that speakers must possess in order to make successful language performance possible.

It can easily be demonstrated that a conscious knowledge of formal grammar is not a necessary condition for the acquisition of fluent language skills. On the other hand, the belief that exposure to pedagogical 'rules of grammar' can only hinder the acquisition of fluent language skills is almost certainly based on an oversimplified view of language structure and of the language learning process. Since there is good reason to believe that the use of language involves rule-based generalizations, it would seem that a theory of language learning should make provision not only for simple associative operations but also for the functioning of abstract grammatical rules. There certainly seems to be a strong case for requiring that teaching grammars be based on an adequate theory of language learning, and that languages be taught in a manner consistent with what we can infer about the nature of a native speaker's knowledge of his language.

It should help to remove a possible source of misunderstanding if we make a clear distinction between formal grammars and practical grammars. Formal grammars are concerned with language competence, i.e. they are designed to provide, in a highly abstract and systematic way, a full specification of the knowledge about language structure that underlies a native speaker's performance. Practical grammars, of which teaching grammars are a particular type, consist of a selection of data drawn from an underlying formal grammar according to rather vague principles of convenience and practical usefulness which are entirely different from the principles that underlie a formal grammar. The advantage of practical grammars lies in the fact that they provide a straight-forward representation of 'surface structure' and lend themselves readily to informal scanning and look-up procedures. On the other hand, the very simplicity which makes a pedagogical grammar easy to use in the classroom usually means that such grammars are bound to omit a great deal of information about the way in which sentences are derived from underlying rules, and the way in which different types of sentences are related to one another in deep structure. A formal grammar provides this information, but has the major disadvantage, from a teaching point of view, that it is too complex to be easily used as a source of reference.

The problem—essentially a practical one—is to decide how much of the formal grammar we can allow to become overt in the teaching grammar at a given stage without endangering the pedagogical validity of the presentation. If we assume for our purposes that 'formal grammar' means the same thing as transformational grammar as defined and elaborated by Chomsky, there seem to be three courses open to us: (1) bring about a reconciliation between the teaching grammar and the formal grammar by writing a transformational teaching text; (2) maintain a sharp distinction between the transformational competence model and the surface structure teaching model in the hope that the underlying rules will be inferred by the student without having to be overtly specified; (3) devise an eclectic teaching model by retaining the surface structure as the basic mode of presentation, but incorporating deep structure insights whenever this can be done without incurring too many abstract rules.

The first alternative is only possible in the case of a teaching grammar designed for advanced native speakers, whose practical mastery of the language is complete and for whom transformational grammar is a formalization of intuitively known facts rather than a source of primary language material. In the case of foreign students we cannot safely assume any intuitively known facts about the language being learned. We cannot take seriously the suggestion that an L_2 classroom presentation should be subject to the formal constraints of transformational theory, because this would mean that we must teach abstract phrase designations before we teach actual sentences, and that new material must be taught through the application of highly complex rules. The second alternative is the one that has been usually adopted in so-called 'structural' syllabuses, but such syllabuses fail to incorporate a great deal of information about language structure which is relevant to the task of language learning. The third alternative seems to be a practical solution for the teacher who would like to incorporate into his teaching some of the insights of a formal grammar without having to adopt a complex apparatus of rules in its entirety. In this case, the rules of the formal grammar will underlie what we teach in the classroom, but the rules will not necessarily be overt in our teaching. One advantage of this proposal is that we will not have to worry about the effect of transformational theory on the sequence of grading in the classroom. Grading will be clearly established as a function of the practical grammar and will not be subject to formal constraints. For example, the fact that *the big car* is derived from an underlying relative *the car which is big* in the formal grammar does not mean that we must introduce the relative before the Adjective+Noun construction when we are preparing a series of lessons for the classroom.

A transformational grammar must achieve maximum economy in its use of rules, and it must generate all and only the well-formed sentences of the language. In order to meet these requirements, the rules must be absolutely explicit. Every step in the derivation of sentences must be fully and accurately described, and there can be no gaps in the formal chain of reasoning. Consequently, a knowledge of transformational grammar serves as a useful check, enabling us to pinpoint the weak spots—the vague generalizations and the unwarranted assumptions—in an informal presentation. Further, the requirement that transformational grammar should achieve the maximum degree of economy in the use of rules leads linguists to search constantly for more concise ways of ordering the material in a grammar. This results in the discovery of underlying regularities which are not necessarily apparent from an examination of surface structure alone, but which may prove to have pedagogical value if the insights are incorporated into a teaching text.

In this final paper Chomsky expresses his doubts whether there can be any direct application in language teaching of the insights achieved in linguistics and psychology. However, four notions are discussed which may be relevant to language teaching: the creative aspect of language use, the abstractness of linguistic representation, the universality of underlying linguistic structure, and the role of intrinsic organization in cognitive processes. These topics indicate the change of emphasis in linguistic studies which has come about as a result of Chomsky's work. The current centre of interest is not the organization of language data so much as the nature of the organizing power that is capable of handling such data. This organizing power, which Chomsky calls 'underlying language competence', gives a human speaker the unique ability to create new sentences which he has never used before, and to understand new sentences which he has never heard before. It is true that most teachers are not directly interested in grammar as an algorithm or a sentence-generating machine, but the current change of emphasis in grammatical studies affects everyone who is concerned with the study of language, in whatever capacity. As linguists, we find ourselves led away from an exclusive preoccupation with patterns of physical data in order to speculate about the internal logic of language structure, and the nature of the knowledge which enables a learner to achieve a creative control of language. As teachers, we are no longer interested solely in what a student says or writes; we are interested in using this physical evidence as a means of making inferences about what the student knows. In other words, we are no longer content merely because a student can give the correct response to a specific stimulus in a controlled repetition or substitution exercise; in addition, we want to satisfy ourselves that by giving the right response the student has really learned something about the language. [A, B]]

7.2 *Implications for language teaching*

I should like to make it clear from the outset that I am participating in this conference* not as an expert on any aspect of the teaching of languages, but rather as someone whose primary concern is with the structure of language and, more generally, the nature of cognitive processes. Furthermore, I am, frankly, rather sceptical about the significance, for the teaching of languages, of such insights and under-

* 'This paper was originally read at the Northeast Conference on the Teaching of Foreign Languages, 1965.' [A, B]

standing as have been attained in linguistics and psychology. Certainly the teacher of language would do well to keep informed of progress and discussion in these fields, and the efforts of linguists and psychologists to approach the problems of language teaching from a principled point of view are extremely worth while, from an intellectual as well as a social point of view. Still, it is difficult to believe that either linguistics or psychology has achieved a level of theoretical understanding that might enable it to support a 'technology' of language teaching. Both fields have made significant progress in recent decades, and, furthermore, both draw on centuries of careful thought and study. These disciplines are, at present, in a state of flux and agitation. What seemed to be well-established doctrine a few years ago may now be the subject of extensive debate. Although it would be difficult to document this generalization, it seems to me that there has been a significant decline, over the past ten or fifteen years, in the degree of confidence in the scope and security of foundations in both psychology and linguistics. I personally feel that this decline in confidence is both healthy and realistic. But it should serve as a warning to teachers that suggestions from the 'fundamental disciplines' must be viewed with caution and scepticism.

Within psychology, there are now many who would question the view that the basic principles of learning are well understood. Long accepted principles of association and reinforcement, gestalt principles, the theory of concept formation as it has emerged in modern investigation, all of these have been sharply challenged in theoretical as well as experimental work. To me it seems that these principles are not merely inadequate but probably misconceived—that they deal with marginal aspects of acquisition of knowledge and leave the central core of the problem untouched. In particular, it seems to me impossible to accept the view that linguistic behaviour is a matter of habit, that it is slowly acquired by reinforcement, association, and generalization, or that linguistic concepts can be specified in terms of a space of elementary, physically defined 'criterial attributes'. Language is not a 'habit structure'. Ordinary linguistic behaviour characteristically involves innovation, formation of new sentences and new patterns in accordance with rules of great abstractness and intricacy. This is true both of the speaker, who constructs new utterances appropriate to the occasion, and of the hearer who must analyse and interpret these novel structures. There are no known principles of association or reinforcement, and no known sense of 'generalization' that can begin to account for this characteristic 'creative' aspect of normal language use. The new utterances that are produced and interpreted in the daily use of language are 'similar' to those that constitute the past experience of speaker and hearer only in that they are determined, in their form and interpretation, by the same system of abstract underlying rules. There is no theory of association or generalization capable of accounting for this fact, and it would, I think, be a fundamental misunderstanding to seek such a theory, since the explanation very likely lies along different lines. The simple concepts of ordinary language (such concepts as 'human being' or 'knife' or 'useful', etc., or, for that matter, the concept 'grammatical sentence') cannot be specified in terms of a space of physical attributes, as in the concept formation paradigm. There is, correspondingly, no obvious analogy between the experimental results obtained in studies of concept formation and the actual processes that seem to underlie language learning.

Evidently, such an evaluation of the relevance of psychological theory to language acquisition requires justification, and it is far from uncontroversial. Nor will I attempt, within the framework of this paper, to supply any such justification. My point simply is that the relevance of psychological theory to acquisition of language is a highly dubious and questionable matter, subject to much controversy and plagued with uncertainties of all sorts. The applied psychologist and the teacher must certainly draw what suggestions and hints they can from psychological research, but they would be well advised to do so with the constant realization of how fragile and tentative are the principles of the underlying discipline.

Turning to linguistics, we find much the same situation. Linguists have had their share in perpetuating the myth that linguistic behaviour is 'habitual' and that a fixed stock of 'patterns' is acquired through practice and used as the basis for 'analogy'. These views could be maintained only as long as grammatical description was sufficiently vague and imprecise. As soon as an attempt is made to give a careful and precise account of the rules of sentence formation, the rules of phonetic organization, or the rules of sound-meaning correspondence in a language, the inadequacy of such an approach becomes apparent. What is more, the fundamental concepts of linguistic description have been subjected to serious critique. The principles of phonemic analysis, for example, have recently been called into question, and the status of the concept 'phoneme' is very much in doubt. For that matter, there are basic, unsolved problems concerning even the phonetic representations used as a basis for analysis of form in structural linguistics. Whereas a decade ago it would have been almost universally assumed that a phonetic representation is simply a record of physical fact, there is now considerable evidence that what the linguist takes to be a phonetic transcription is determined, in nontrivial ways, by the syntactic structure of the language, and that it is, to this extent, independent of the physical signal. I think there are by now very few linguists who believe that it is possible to arrive at the phonological or syntactic structure of a language by systematic application of 'analytic procedures' of segmentation and classification, although fifteen or twenty years ago such a view was not only widely accepted but was also supported by significant results and quite plausible argument.

I would like to emphasize again that this questioning of fundamental principles is a very healthy phenomenon that has led to important advances and will undoubtedly continue to do so. It is, in fact, characteristic of any living subject. But it must be recognized that well-established theory, in fields like psychology and linguistics, is extremely limited in scope. The applications of physics to engineering may not be seriously affected by even the most deep-seated revolution in the foundations of physics, but the applications of psychology or linguistics to language teaching, such as they are, may be gravely affected by changing conceptions in these fields, since the body of theory that resists substantial modification is fairly small.

In general, the willingness to rely on 'experts' is a frightening aspect of contemporary political and social life. Teachers, in particular, have a responsibility to make sure that ideas and proposals are evaluated on their merits, and not passively accepted on grounds of authority, real or presumed. The field of language teaching is no exception. It is possible—even likely—that principles of psychology and linguistics, and research in these disciplines, may supply insights useful to the language teacher. But this must be demonstrated, and cannot be presumed. It is the language teacher himself who must validate or refute any specific proposal. There is very little in psychology or linguistics that he can accept on faith.

I will not try to develop any specific proposals relating to the teaching of languages—as I mentioned before, because I am not competent to do so. But there are certain tendencies and developments within linguistics and psychology that may have some potential impact on the teaching of language. I think these can be usefully summarized under four main headings: the 'creative' aspect of language use; the abstractness of linguistic representation; the universality of underlying linguistic structure; the role of intrinsic organization in cognitive processes. I would like to say just a few words about each of these topics.

The most obvious and characteristic property of normal linguistic behaviour is that it is stimulus-free and innovative. Repetition of fixed phrases is a rarity; it is only under exceptional and quite uninteresting circumstances that one can seriously consider how 'situational context' determines what is said, even in probabilistic terms. The notion that linguistic behaviour consists of 'responses' to 'stimuli' is as much a myth as the idea that it is a matter of habit and generalization. To maintain such assumptions in the face of the actual facts, we must deprive the terms 'stimulus' and 'response' (similarly 'habit' and 'generalization') of any technical or precise meaning. This property of being innovative and stimulus-free is what I refer to by the term 'creative aspect of language use'. It is a property of language that was described in the seventeenth century and that serves as one cornerstone for classical linguistic theory, but that has gradually been forgotten in the development of modern linguistics, much to its detriment. Any theory of language must come to grips with this fundamental property of normal language use. A necessary but not sufficient step towards dealing with this problem is to recognize that the native speaker of a language has internalized a 'generative grammar'—a system of rules that can be used in new and untried combinations to form new sentences and to assign semantic interpretations to new sentences. Once this fact has become clear, the immediate task of the linguist is likewise clarified. He must try to discover the rules of this generative grammar and the underlying principles on the basis of which it is organized.

The native speaker of a language has internalized a generative grammar in the sense just described, but he obviously has no awareness of this fact or of the properties of this grammar. The problem facing the linguist is to discover what constitutes unconscious, latent knowledge—to bring to light what is now sometimes called the speaker's intrinsic 'linguistic competence'. A generative grammar of a language is a theory of the speaker's competence. If correct, it expresses the principles that determine the intrinsic correlation of sound and meaning in the language in question. It thus serves as one component of a theory that can accommodate the characteristic creative aspect of language use.

When we try to construct explicit, generative grammars and investigate their properties, we discover at once many inadequacies in traditional and modern linguistic descriptions. It is often said that no complete generative grammar has ever been written for any language, the implication being that this 'new-fangled' approach suffers in comparison with older and well-established approaches to language description, in this respect. The statement concerning generative grammar is quite accurate; the conclusion, if intended, reveals a serious misunderstanding. Even the small fragments of generative grammars that now exist are incomparably greater in explicit coverage than traditional or structuralist descriptions, and it is important to be aware of this fact. A generative grammar is simply one that gives explicit rules that determine the structure of sentences, their phonetic form, and their semantic interpretation. The limitations of generative grammar are the limitations of our knowledge, in these areas. Where traditional or structuralist descriptions are correct, they can immediately be incorporated into generative grammars. In so far as these descriptions merely list examples of various kinds and make remarks (which may be interesting and suggestive) about them, then they cannot be directly incorporated into generative grammars. In other words, a traditional or structuralist description can be immediately incorporated into a generative grammar to the extent that it is correct and does not rely on the 'intelligence of the reader' and his 'linguistic intuition'. The limitations of generative grammar, then, are a direct reflection of the limitations of correctness and explicitness in earlier linguistic work.

A serious investigation of generative grammars quickly shows that the rules that determine the form of sentences and their interpretations are not only intricate but also quite abstract, in the sense that the structures they manipulate are related to physical fact only in a remote way, by a long chain of interpretative rules. This is as true on the level of phonology as it is on the level of syntax and semantics, and it is this fact that has led to the questioning both of structuralist principles and of the tacitly assumed psychological theory that underlies them. It is because of the abstractness of linguistic representations that one is forced, in my opinion, to reject not only the analytic procedures of modern linguistics, with their reliance on segmentation and classification, but also principles of association and generalization that have been discussed and studied in empiricist psychology. Although such phenomena as association and generalization, in the sense of psychological theory and philosophical speculation, may indeed exist, it is difficult to see how they have any bearing on the acquisition or use of language. If our current conceptions of generative grammar are at all accurate, then the structures manipulated and the principles operating in these grammars are not related to given sensory phenomena in any way describable in the terms that empiricist psychology offers, and what principles it suggests simply have no relation to the facts that demand explanation.

If it is correct that the underlying principles of generative grammars cannot be acquired through experience and training, then they must be part of the intellectual organization which is a prerequisite for language acquisition. They must, therefore, be universal properties, properties of any generative grammar. These are, then, two distinct ways of approaching what is clearly the most fundamental question of linguistic science, namely, the question of linguistic universals. One way is by an investigation of a wide range of languages. Any hypothesis as to the nature of linguistic universals must meet the empirical condition that it is not falsified by any natural language, any language acquired and used by humans in the normal way. But there is also another and, for the time being, somewhat more promising way of studying the problem of universals. This is by deep investigation of a particular language, investigation directed towards establishing underlying principles of organization of great abstractness in this language. Where such principles can be established, we must account for their existence. One plausible hypothesis is that they are innate, therefore, universal. Another plausible hypothesis is that they are acquired through experience and training. Either hypothesis can be made precise; each will then be meaningful and worthy of attention. We can refute the former by showing that other aspects of this language or properties of other languages are inconsistent with it. We can refute the latter by showing that it does not yield the structures that we must presuppose to account for linguistic competence. In general, it seems to me quite impossible to account for many deep-seated aspects of language on the basis of training or experience, and that therefore one must search for an explanation for them in terms of intrinsic intellectual organization. An almost superstitious refusal to consider this proposal seriously has, in my opinion, enormously set back both linguistics and psychology. For the present, it seems to me that there is no more reason for assuming that the basic principles of grammar are learned than there is for making a comparable assumption about, let us say, visual perception. There is, in short, no more reason to suppose that a person learns that English has a generative grammar of a very special and quite explicitly definable sort than there is to suppose that the same person learns to analyse the visual field in terms of line, angle, motion, solidity, persons with faces, etc.

Turning then to the last of the four topics mentioned above, I think that one of the most important current developments in psychology and neurophysiology is the investigation of intrinsic organization in cognition. In the particular case of language, there is good reason to believe that even the identification of the phonetic form of a sentence presupposes at least a partial syntactic analysis, so that the rules of the generative grammar may be brought into play even in identifying the signal. This view is opposed to the hypothesis that phonetic representation is determined by the signal completely, and that the perceptual analysis proceeds from formal signals to interpretation, a hypothesis which, I understand, has been widely quoted in discussion of language teaching. The role of the generative grammar in perception is paralleled by the role of the universal grammar—the system of invariant underlying principles of linguistic organization—in acquisition of language. In each case, it seems to me that the significance of the intrinsic organization is very great indeed, and that the primary goal of linguistic and psychological investigation of language must be to determine and characterize it.

I am not sure that this very brief discussion of some of the leading ideas of much current research has been sufficiently clear to be either informative or convincing. Once again, I would like to stress that the implications of these ideas for language teaching are far from clear to me. It is a rather dubious undertaking to try to predict the course of development of any field, but, for what it is worth, it seems to me likely that questions of this sort will dominate research in the coming years, and, to hazard a further guess, that this research will show that certain highly abstract and highly specific principles of organization are characteristic of all human languages, are intrinsic rather than acquired, play a central role in perception as well as in production of sentences, and provide the basis for the creative aspect of language use.

'Linguistic theory' (*1966*), *43–9*

Bibliography

References

Bever, T. G., and Rosenbaum, P. *Two Studies on Syntax and Semantics*. Bedford. Mass.: Mitre Corporation Technical Reports.

Bloch, B. (1940). 'Phonemic overlapping.' *American Speech*, **16**, 278–84. Reprinted in M. Joos, *Readings in Linguistics I*.

Bloch, B. (1948). 'A set of postulates for phonemic analysis.' *Language*, **24**, 3–46.

Bloch, B. (1950). 'Studies in colloquial Japanese IV: phonemics.' *Language*, **26**, 86–125. Reprinted in M. Joos, *Readings in Linguistics I*.

Bloomfield, M. (1963). 'A grammatical approach to personification allegory.' *Modern Philology*, **60**, 161–71.

Chomsky, N. (1965). *Aspects of the Theory of Syntax*.

Chomsky, N., and Halle, M. (1968). *The Sound Pattern of English*.

Fillmore, C. J. (1963). 'The position of embedding transformations in a grammar.' *Word*, **19**, 208–31.

Fodor, J. A., and Katz, J. J. (eds.) (1964). *The Structure of Language: Readings in the Philosophy of Language*. Englewood Cliffs, N. J.: Prentice-Hall.

Halle, M. (1961). 'On the role of simplicity in linguistic descriptions.' In R. Jakobson (ed.), *Structure of Language and its Mathematical Aspects, Proc. 12th Symp. in App. Math.*, Providence, R.I.: American Mathematical Society, 89–94.

Halle, M. (1962). 'Phonology in generative grammar.' *Word*, **18**, 54–72.

Held, R., and Freedman, S. J. (1963). 'Plasticity in human sensorimotor control.' *Science*, **142**, 455–62.

Held, R., and Hein, A. (1963). 'Movement-produced stimulation in the development of visually guided behavior.' *J. of Comparative and Physiological Psychology*, **56**, 872–6.

Humboldt, W. von (1836). *Über die Verschiedenheit des Menschlichen Sprachbaues*, Berlin. Republished, Darmstadt: Claasen and Roether, 1949.

Hume, D. (1748). *An Enquiry Concerning Human Understanding*.

Jakobson, R., Fant, C. G. M., and Halle, M. (1951). *Preliminaries to Speech Analysis*, M.I.T. Acoustics Lab., Cambridge, Mass.: M.I.T. Press, 1963.

Jakobson, R., and Halle, M. (1956). *Fundamentals of Language*. The Hague: Mouton.

Joos, M. (ed.) (1966). *Readings in Linguistics I*, 4th edition. Chicago: University of Chicago Press.

Katz, J. J., and Fodor, J. A. (1963). 'The structure of a semantic theory.' *Language*, **39**, 170–210. Reprinted in Fodor and Katz, *The Structure of Language*.

Katz, J. J. (1964). 'Analyticity and contradiction in natural languages.' In Fodor and Katz, *The Structure of Language*.

Katz, J. J., and Postal, P. M. (1964). *An Integrated Theory of Linguistic Descriptions* (Research Monographs No. 26). Cambridge, Mass.: M.I.T. Press.

Lees, R. B. (1960). *The Grammar of English Nominalisations*. Bloomington, Ind.: Research Center in Anthropology, Folklore and Linguistics.

Leibniz, G. W. *New Essays Concerning Human Understanding*. Translated by A. G. Langley, LaSalle, Ill.: Open Court, 1949.

Lemmon, W. B., and Patterson, G. H. (1964). 'Depth perception in sheep.' *Science*, **145**, p. 835.

Liberman, A. M., Delattre, P., and Cooper, F. S. (1952). 'The role of selected stimulus variables in the perception of unvoiced stop consonants.' *American J. of Psychology*, **65**, 497–516.

Miller, G. A., and Norman, D. A. (1964). *Research on the Use of Formal Languages in the Behavioural Sciences*. Semi-annual Technical Report, Department of Defense, Advanced Research Projects Agency, January-June 1964, **10–11**. Cambridge, Mass.: Harvard University, Center for Cognitive Studies.

Postal, P. M. (1968). *Aspects of Phonological Theory*. New York: Harper and Row.

Quine, W. V. (1960). *Word and Object*. Cambridge, Mass.: M.I.T. Press, and New York: Wiley.

Reibal, D. A., and Schane, S. A. (1969). *Modern Studies in English*. Englewood Cliffs, N.J., Prentice-Hall.

Sapir, E. (1925). 'Sound patterns in language.' *Language*, **1**, 37–51. Reprinted in D. G. Mandelbaum (ed.), *Selected Writings of Edward Sapir*. Berkeley: University of California Press, 1949.

Sapir, E. (1933). 'La réalité psychologique des phonèmes.' *J. de psychologie normale et pathologique*, 247–65. Reprinted in D. G. Mandelbaum (ed.), *Selected Writings of Edward Sapir*. Berkeley: University of California Press, 1949.

Saussure, F. de (1916). *Cours de Linguistique General*. Paris: Payot. English translation: Wade Baskin, *Course in General Linguistics*, New York, Philosophical Library, 1959.

Schatz, C. D. (1954). 'The role of context in the perception of stops.' *Language*, **30**, 47.

Skinner, B. F. (1957). *Verbal Behavior*. New York: Appleton-Century-Crofts.

Sweet, H. (1877). *A Handbook of Phonetics*. Oxford: Clarendon Press.

Wilson, J. C. (1926). *Statement and Inference*, Vol. I. Oxford: Clarendon Press.

Noam Chomsky: Select Bibliography

1951. 'Morphophonemics of Modern Hebrew.' Unpublished Master's thesis, University of Pennsylvania.

1953. 'Systems of syntactic analysis.' *J. Symbolic Logic*, **18**, 242–56.

1955. 'Logical syntax and semantics: their linguistic relevance.' *Language*, **31**, 36–45.

The Logical Structure of Linguistic Theory. Mimeographed, M.I.T. Library, Cambridge, Mass.

'Transformational Analysis.' Ph.D. dissertation, University of Pennsylvania.

Semantic Considerations in Grammar. Monograph No. 8, Georgetown University Institute of Languages and Linguistics, Washington D.C.

1956. 'On accent and juncture in English', with M. Halle and F. Lukoff. In M. Halle, H. Lunt, and H. MacLean (eds.), *For Roman Jakobson*, 65–80. The Hague: Mouton.

'Three models for the description of language.' *I.R.E. Transactions on Information Theory*, Vol. IT-2, 113–24. Reprinted, with corrections, in R. D. Luce, R. Bush and E. Galanter (eds.), *Readings in Mathematical Psychology*, Vol. II. New York: Wiley, 1963.

1957. *Syntactic Structures.* The Hague: Mouton.

Review of Hockett, Manual of Phonology. *Int. J. American Linguistics*, **23**, 223–34.

Review of Jakobson and Halle, Fundamentals of Language. *Int. J. American Linguistics*, **23**, 234–42.

'Logical structures in language.' *American Documentation*, Vol. 8, no. 4, 284–91.

1958. 'Finite state languages', with G. A. Miller. *Information and Control*, **1**, 91–112. Reprinted in R. D. Luce, R. Bush and E. Galanter (eds.), *Readings in Mathematical Psychology*, Vol. II. New York: Wiley, 1963.

'Linguistics, logic, psychology and computers.' *Computer Programming and Artificial Intelligence*, 429–56. Lectures given at University of Michigan, 1948.

1959. Review of Skinner, Verbal Behavior. *Language*, **35**, 26–58. Reprinted in Fodor and Katz, *The Structure of Language*.

Review of Greenberg, Essays in Linguistics. *Word*, **15**, 202–18.

'On certain formal properties of grammars.' *Information and Control*, **2**, 137–67. Reprinted in R. D. Luce, R. Bush, and E. Galanter (eds.), *Readings in Mathematical Psychology*, Vol. II. New York: Wiley, 1963.

'A note on phrase structure grammars.' *Information and Control*, **2**, 393–5.

1960. 'The morphophonemics of English', with M. Halle. *Quarterly Progress Report No. 58*, Cambridge, Mass: Research Lab. of Electronics, 275–81.

1961. 'On the notion "rule of grammar".' In R. Jakobson (ed.), *Structure of Language and its Mathematical Aspect, Proc. 12th Symp. in App. Math.* Providence, R. I.: American Mathematical Society, 6–24. Reprinted in Fodor and Katz, *The Structure of Language*.

'Some methodological remarks on generative grammar.' *Word*, **17**, 219–39. Reprinted in part in Fodor and Katz, *The Structure of Language*.

1962. 'Explanatory models in linguistics.' In E. Nagel, P. Suppes and A. Tarski, *Logic, Methodology and Philosophy of Science: Proc. of the 1960 Int.*

Congress. Stanford, California: Stanford University Press, 528–50.
'The logical basis of linguistic theory.' *Preprints of the Ninth Int. Congress of Linguists*, Cambridge, Mass., 509–74. Reprinted in Fodor and Katz, *The Structure of Language* as 'Current Issues in Linguistic Theory'.
'Context-free grammars and pushdown storage', *RLE Quarterly Progress Report No. 65*. Cambridge, Mass.: M.I.T.
'A transformational approach to syntax.' In A. A. Hill (ed.), *Proc. of the 1958 Conference on Problems of Linguistic Analysis in English*, 124–48, Austin, Texas. Reprinted in Fodor and Katz, *The Structure of Language*.

1963. 'The algebraic theory of context-free languages', with M. P. Schützenberger. In P. Braffort and D. Hirschbert (eds.), *Computer Programming and Formal Systems*, 119–61, *Studies in Logic Series*. Amsterdam: North-Holland.
'Perception and language.' In Wartofsky (ed.), *Boston Studies in the Philosophy of Science*, 199–205. Reidel, Dordrecht-Holland.
'Formal properties of grammars.' In R. D. Luce, R. Bush, and E. Galanter (eds.), *Handbook of Mathematical Psychology*, Vol. II. New York: Wiley, 1963, 323–418.
'Introduction to the formal analysis of natural languages', with G. A. Miller. *Ibid.*, 269–322.
'Finitary models of language users', with G. A. Miller. *Ibid.*, 419–91.

1964. *Current Issues in Linguistic Theory*. The Hague: Mouton. A revised and expanded version of the paper in the *Ninth Int. Congress of Linguists* Proceedings, 1962.
'Formal discussion: the development of grammar in child language.' In Ursula Bellugi and Roger Brown (eds.), *The Acquisition of Language*, *Monographs of the Society for Research in Child Development*, Vol. 29, no. 1. Purdue University, Indiana.

1965. 'Some controversial questions in phonological theory', with M. Halle. *Journal of Linguistics*, Vol. 1, no. 2, 97–138.
Aspects of the Theory of Syntax. Cambridge, Mass.: M.I.T. Press.

1966. *Cartesian Linguistics*. New York and London: Harper & Row.
Topics in the Theory of Generative Grammar. The Hague: Mouton. Also printed in T. A. Sebeok (ed.), *Current Trends in Linguistics*, Vol. III: *Linguistic Theory*. The Hague: Mouton.
'The current scene in linguistics: present directions.' In *College English*, 27, 587–95. Reprinted in Reibal and Schane, *Modern Studies in English*.
'Linguistic theory.' In Robert G. Mead, Jr. (ed.), *Language Teaching: Broader Contexts*, Northeast Conference Reports.

1967. 'The formal nature of language.' Appendix to E. H. Lenneberg, *Biological Foundations of Language*. New York: Wiley.

'Some general properties of phonological rules.' *Language*, 43, no. 1.
'The general properties of language.' In P. L. Darley (ed.), *Brain Mechanisms Underlying Speech and Language*, Proceedings of a Conference held at Princeton, N.J., 9–12 November 1965. New York: Grune & Stratton, 73–81.

1968. *The Sound Pattern of English*, with M. Halle. New York: Harper & Row.
'A universal grammar: a discussion with Stuart Hampshire and Alasdair MacIntyre.' *The Listener*, Vol. 29, no. 2044, Thursday, 30 May 1968.
Language and Mind. New York: Harcourt Brace.

1969. 'Linguistics and philosophy.' In S. Hook (ed.), *Language and Philosophy*. New York University Press (New York University Institute of Philosophy Symposium), 51–94.
'Knowledge of language', excerpted from the first John Locke Lecture, Oxford, 29 April 1969. London: *Times Literary Supplement*, 15 May 1969.
'Some observations on the teaching of language.' *The Pedagogic Reporter*, Vol. 21, no. 1, 5–6, 13.
'Form and meaning in natural language.' In John D. Roslansky (ed.), *Communication*. Amsterdam: North-Holland.

1970. 'Remarks on nominalisation.' In R. Jacobs and P. Rosenbaum (eds.), *Readings in Transformational Grammar*. Waltham, Mass.: Blaisdell.
'Phonology and reading.' In H. Levin and Joanna P. Williams (eds.), *Basic Studies in Reading*. New York: Basic Books.
'Problems of explanation in linguistics.' In R. Borger and F. Cioffi (eds.), *Explanations in the Behavioural Sciences*. New York: Cambridge University Press.

Forthcoming

'Deep structure, surface structure and semantic interpretation.' In R. Jakobson and S. Kawamoto (eds.), *Studies in General and Oriental Linguistics*, Commemorative Volume for Dr. Shiro Hattori. Tokyo: TEC Corporation for Language Research.
'Some observations on the problems of semantic analysis in natural languages.' In *Sign, Language, Culture*, The Hague: Mouton.

Further Reading

Abercrombie, David (1967). *Elements of General Phonetics*. Edinburgh: Edinburgh University Press and Chicago: Aldine.
Bach, E. (1964). *An Introduction to Transformational Grammars*. New York: Holt, Rinehart, Winston.
Bach, E., and Harms, R. T. (1968). *Universals in Linguistic Theory*. New York: Holt, Rinehart, Winston.
Bloomfield, L. (1933). *Language*. New York: Holt, Rinehart, Winston; and London: Allen & Unwin, 1935.

Bolinger, Dwight (1968). *Aspects of Language*. New York: Harcourt Brace.

Fodor, J. A., and Katz, J. J. (eds.) (1964). *The Structure of Language: Readings in the Philosophy of Language*. Englewood Cliffs, N.J.: Prentice-Hall.

Gleason, H. A. (1961). *An Introduction to Descriptive Linguistics*. 2nd revised edition. New York: Holt, Rinehart, Winston.

Hamp, E. P., Householder, F. W., and Austerlitz, R. (eds.) (1966). *Readings in Linguistics II*. Companion volume to M. Joos, *Readings in Linguistics I*. Chicago: University of Chicago Press.

Harms, R. T. (1968). *Introduction to Phonological Theory*. Englewood Cliffs, N.J.: Prentice-Hall.

Harris, Z. S. (1951). *Methods in Structural Linguistics*. Chicago: University of Chicago Press. Reprinted as *Structural Linguistics*, 1961.

Harris, Z. S. (1957). 'Co-occurrence and transformation in linguistic structure.' *Language*, **33**, 293–340. Reprinted in Fodor and Katz, 1964.

Hockett, C. F. (1958). *A Course in Modern Linguistics*. New York: Macmillan.

Jacobs, R. A., and Rosenbaum, P. S. (1968). *English Transformational Grammar*. Waltham, Mass: Blaisdell.

Jacobs, R. A., and Rosenbaum, P. S. (eds.) (1970). *Readings in Transformational Grammar*. Waltham, Mass: Blaisdell.

Jakobson, R., and Halle, M. (1956). *Fundamentals of Language*. The Hague: Mouton.

Jones, Daniel (1950). *The Phoneme: Its Nature and Use*. Cambridge: Heffer.

Joos, Martin (ed.) (1966). *Readings in Linguistics I*, 4th edition. Companion volume to Hamp, Householder, and Austerlitz, *Readings in Linguistics II*. Chicago: University of Chicago Press.

Katz, J. J. (1964). 'Mentalism in linguistics.' *Language*, **40**, 124–37.

Katz, J. J., and Postal, P. M. (1964). *An Integrated Theory of Linguistic Descriptions*. (Research Monographs, 26.) Cambridge, Mass.: M.I.T. Press.

Koutsoudas, Andreas (1967). *Writing Transformational Grammars*. New York: McGraw-Hill.

Lees, R. B. (1957). Review of Chomsky, Syntactic Structures. *Language*, **33**, 375–407.

Lenneberg, E. H. (1967). *Biological Foundations of Language*. New York: Wiley.

Longacker, R. W. (1967). *Language and Its Structure: Some Fundamental Linguistic Concepts*. New York: Harcourt Brace.

Lyons, John (1968). *Introduction to Theoretical Linguistics*. Cambridge: Cambridge University Press.

Lyons, John, and Wales, R. J. (eds.) (1966). *Psycholinguistics Papers: Proceedings of the Edinburgh Conference*. Edinburgh: Edinburgh University Press.

Lyons, John (1970). *Chomsky*. London: Fontana Modern Masters.

Matthews, P. H. (1967). Review of Chomsky, Aspects of the Theory of Syntax. *Journal of Linguistics*, **3**, 119–52.

Menyuk, Paula (1969). *Sentences Children Use*. Cambridge, Mass.

Nida, E. A. (1949). *Morphology: The Descriptive Analysis of Words.* 2nd edition. Ann Arbor: University of Michigan Press.

Oldfield, R. C., and Marshall, J. C. (eds.) (1968). *Language: Selected Readings.* Harmondsworth: Penguin.

Pike, K. L. (1947). *Phonemics: A Technique for Reducing Languages to Writing.* Ann Arbor: University of Michigan Press.

Postal, P. M. (1964). *Constituent Structure: A Study of Contemporary Models of Syntactic Description.* Bloomington, Ind.: Research Center in Anthropology, Folklore and Linguistics.

Postal, P. M. (1968). *Aspects of Phonological Theory.* New York: Harper & Row.

Reibel, D. A., and Schane, S. A. (1969). *Modern Studies in English.* Englewood Cliffs, N.J.: Prentice-Hall.

Roberts, Paul (1964). *English Syntax.* New York: Harcourt Brace.

Ruwet, Nicolas (1968). *Introduction à la Grammaire Générative.* Paris: Libraire Plon.

Saporta, S. (ed.) (1961). *Psycholinguistics: A Book of Readings.* New York: Holt, Rinehart, Winston.

Saussure, F. de (1916). *Cours de Linguistique Général.* Paris: Payot. English translation: Wade Baskin, *Course in General Linguistics.* New York: Philosophical Library, 1959.

Seuren, Pieter A. M. (1969). *Operators and Nucleus.* Cambridge: Cambridge University Press.

Smith, Frank, and Miller, G. A. (eds.) (1966). *The Genesis of Language.* Cambridge, Mass.: M.I.T. Press.

Thomas, Owen (1966). *Transformational Grammar and the Teacher of English.* New York: Holt, Rinehart, Winston.